D1098085

THE STRUGGLE FOR SOVEREIGNTY IN ENGLAND

THE STRUGGLE FOR
SOVEREIGNTY IN ENGLAND

From the Reign of Queen Elizabeth
to the Petition of Right

GEORGE L. MOSSE

*"The wisest King did wonder when he espied
the Nobles march on foot, the vassals ride.
His Majesty may wonder more to see
some that would needs be Kings as well as He.
A sad passage of danger to the land
when lower tries to get the upper hand...."*

—VERSES AGAINST THE HOUSE OF COMMONS, 1628
ELLESMERE MSS. 7728

1968
OCTAGON BOOKS, INC.
New York

Reprinted 1968
by special arrangement with the Michigan State University Press

OCTAGON BOOKS, INC.
175 FIFTH AVENUE
NEW YORK, N. Y. 10010

LIBRARY OF CONGRESS CATALOG CARD NUMBER: 68-22299

Printed in U.S.A. by
NOBLE OFFSET PRINTERS, INC.
NEW YORK 3, N. Y.

Preface

†

THIS WORK WAS ORIGINALLY undertaken at the suggestion of
Professor Charles H. McIlwain of Harvard University. Those
who are familiar with the writings and teachings of this great
scholar will recognize how greatly I have relied upon the contributions which he has made to the understanding of English
political theory. To President W. K. Jordan of Radcliffe Col-
lege I have never looked in vain for aid, guidance, and advice.
Professor Ernest H. Kantorowicz of the University of Cali-
fornia and Professor R. Stuart Hoyt of the State University of
Iowa have most generously put their knowledge of medieval
history at my disposal in the preparation of the study. Without the assistance of Mrs. Margaret Zerby and Mr. Robert E.
Ruigh the completion of the book would have been a much
harder task. The librarians of the Henry E. Huntington Library, the Newberry Library, the Widener Library, the British
Museum and the Libraries of the State University of Iowa have
been generous in facilitating the use of their materials. The Earl
of Leicester kindly granted me access to Sir Edward Coke's
library preserved at Holkham. The editors of *Speculum*,
Medievalia et Humanistica, and the *University of Toronto
Quarterly* have given their permission to use materials from
articles which first appeared in these periodicals.

Webster's Dictionary defines an essay as "a literary composition, analytical or interpretive, dealing with its subject from a more or less limited or personal standpoint." It is as an essay that this work was written and none of those to whom I am so greatly indebted can be held responsible for the analyses and interpretations set forth in this book. It should be noted here, perhaps, that the spelling of all quotations used in this book have been modernized in order to allow for smoother reading. I regret that Margaret Atwood Judson's *The Crisis of the Constitution* appeared too late for me to make as much use of as I would have liked. The fact that Miss Judson's work and this book have different approaches and tend to different conclusions should demonstrate once again the richness of English political thought in the first decades of the seventeenth century.

G.L.M.

Department of History
State University of Iowa
1950

Contents

†

Introduction

THE PROBLEM OF SOVEREIGNTY

†

THE PURPOSE OF THIS ESSAY is to analyze the assimilation of the idea of sovereignty in English constitutional and political thought. In a world where the boundary lines between the rights of individuals and the power of the state are ever in dispute, the development of the idea of sovereignty takes on great significance.

Modern political and constitutional thought inclines toward the notion that sovereignty is the possession of power inherent in that sole organ of the state which cannot be controlled by any other power and which is therefore solely absolute. The giving of law is considered to be one of the essential functions of this absolute authority; John Austin's definition of "law" seems to be the generally accepted one, bound as it is with modern ideas of sovereign power:

Every positive law, or every law strictly or simply so called, is set by a sovereign person, or a sovereign body of persons, to a member or members of the independent political society wherein that person or body is sovereign or supreme.[1]

[1] John Austin, *The Province of Jurisprudence Determined* (London: J. Murray, 1861), p. 169.

And so, whether we live under the rule of a king, a dictator, or a parliament, the rights of the individual are subordinated to the obedience given to the laws of the supreme sovereign authority.

Yet the classic definition of sovereignty, as elaborated in the sixteenth century, envisaged not only a supreme authority but also a government in which certain rights were guaranteed to the subject by a law which was above and without the reach of the sovereign. If this idea of a "limited sovereignty" seems to us to be a contradiction in terms, it is because the struggles for power in modern times have served to obliterate a concept which was a medieval commonplace. It is the destruction of this medieval concept of limitations, even upon so-called sovereign power, which this essay analyzes.

In England, the emergence of the modern idea of sovereignty, as propounded by John Austin, was the result of the struggle for power between king and Parliament which dominated the seventeenth century. At the beginning of the Tudor period we find repeated with monotonous frequency the sentiment that the king should rule by law and not by his absolute power; that his sovereignty was limited by a law which guaranteed the traditional rights of Englishmen. However, by the middle of the next century we find it openly stated that "the power of the sword is and ever has been the foundation of all government." [2] From a concept of legal limitations we have passed to the idea of a commonwealth ruled by force proceeding from the office of a sovereign.

The medieval limitations upon the sovereign were conceived to be largely legal in nature, and it is for that reason that the law must stand in the center of any discussion of the historical evolution of the idea of sovereignty in England. Medieval man believed in the existence of a natural law, which was usually described as the law of God applied to man. The precepts of natural law were of divine origin. This natural law, as men like Sir John Fortescue used it, was no mere pious theory, no polite

[2] Marchamont Nedham, *The Case of the Commonwealth of England Stated etc.* (London, 1650), p. 6.

rhetoric, for it guaranteed the harmony of the commonwealth: it ordained and explained the sociopolitical structure which made the continuance of the state both right and necessary. The limitations upon the sovereign were enshrined here. The ancient laws and the customs of the realm were outside the sovereign's reach, for they were merely the application of this highest body of divine law. Thus law was never "newly made," and it certainly was no mere command of an earthly sovereign. If there were to be adjustments in the traditional customs of the people, these adjustments had to be made jointly by all concerned: by the king with the "concurrent consent" of the people. When Henry VIII declared that

> We at no time stand so high in our estate royal as in time of Parliament; when we as head and you as members, are conjoined and knit together into one body politic. . . .[3]

he was thinking in terms of the medieval ideal of the harmonious commonwealth where sudden changes and inventions were prevented by the law of nature itself and wherein all members of the political structure functioned in unison with a divine and unavoidable natural law. We are here still far removed from James I's image of the king as the patriarch ruling his family.

The emergence of the modern idea of sovereignty meant, therefore, the weakening of that law of nature which gave divine sanction to a commonwealth where both the king as sovereign and the people as subjects were knit together into one body obedient to God's will. Instead of the law of nature, lawyers during the Tudor period began increasingly to speak about the law of reason.

This law of reason was broader than medieval views of the law of nature had been concrete. It was no longer a higher law guaranteeing the limitations upon the sovereign. As Tudor lawyers began to use this concept, it allowed for sovereignty in our modern sense. Christopher St. Germain, in the reign of

[3] Quoted in Charles Howard McIlwain, *The High Court of Parliament and Its Supremacy* (New Haven: Yale University Press, 1910), p. 338.

King Henry VIII, assumed that the king and Parliament together would never do anything against truth or reason—this
despite the fact that they had just invaded the traditional rights
of subjects in a spectacular way by summarily depriving the
monasteries of their land, and, through the Statute of Uses,
transferring the title to land from the customary owners to
those persons who enjoyed its use. The law of reason as a suc-
cessor to the law of nature took on the aspect of a higher law
which, while still being above the sovereign power, yet was
able to upset tradition, allowing new concepts to assert themselves with a hitherto undreamt of impunity.

Even this law of reason was to be challenged as higher law
by the beginning of the seventeenth century. In the quest toward the emergence of an unfettered sovereign power, Roman
ideas could well be used. Roman law was a body of law which
transcended national boundaries and could, therefore, come
forward with the claim to be the real natural law. The concept
of the Roman (or civil) law as a law of last appeal again fur-
thered the emergence of the Austinian concept of sovereignty.
To sixteenth- and seventeenth-century man, the idea of the
king as *legibus solutus* seemed to be the cardinal maxim of the
civil law. This had not always been so, and there were writers,
even in Elizabethan days, who did not see any great contradiction between the civil law and a government of England hallowed by the medieval law of nature. Yet with the growing
identification of civil law and the maxims of absolutism, any
theory which substituted it for the old natural law was bound
to be dangerous to medieval concepts of the English constitution. The changing ideas as to the nature of the higher law of
"last appeal" are consequently of great importance in tracing
the concept of sovereignty, for whether men thought in terms
of "natural law," the "law of reason," or "civil law" was significant in terms of the legal limitations which could be applied
to the sovereign.

The several views of the nature of the higher law reflected,
in turn, upon the view taken of the law of England itself: the
common law. It was the common law which, in actual fact,

cemented the commonwealth of medieval times. It defined the
relationship of the different parts of the state to each other,
and prevented any group or section of the commonwealth from
raising itself above the others and imposing its laws upon the
rest. It was this common law which was merely the reflection
of the law of nature and thus was enshrined "in the bosom of
God." It could only be changed by the body politic, knit together in Parliament, and even then it was matter for dispute
whether Parliamentary statutes could run counter to the precepts of the common law and, through it, to those of the law
of nature itself. Once the law of nature was discarded for the
law of reason on the one hand, or for the Roman law on the
other, the common law of England in turn could no longer
function as a bar to absolute power. Law could then become
an order established by human authority.

The common law has been assigned the cardinal place in this
discussion of the evolution of the idea of sovereignty in England. The controversy which raged around its precepts and its
general nature can best show us the emergence of the new concepts of sovereignty. Moreover, those who sought to stem the
tide toward sovereignty tried to rally behind the common law
as the best remaining shield to protect the liberty of the individual. In an age when both the king and the Parliament were
engaged in a struggle for power, an age which tended to dis-
regard the traditional view of the "body politic, knit together,"
common lawyers like Sir Edward Coke sought to protect liberty against both extremes. Perhaps here we can see the dawn
of a modern liberalism which, like the common lawyers in an
age of competition for sovereignty, tries to preserve a middle
way which is supported as a guarantee of individual liberty
against popular and extremist ideologies. Like many modern
liberals, the common lawyers thought of "rights" in legal rather
than in economic or social terms. A right was guaranteed by
the common law against all powers and was to them vastly different from a privilege granted as a boon by a sovereign. The
development which we are discussing will take us from a society of rights to a society of privileges. What emerges is omni-

competent power. During the course of the English Revolution a pamphleteer stated bluntly: "The question never was whether we should be governed by arbitrary power, but in whose hands it should be." [4]

It is difficult to set chronological limits to a study concerned with the evolution of ideas. The ascendance of Henry Tudor to the throne of England in 1485 marked no break in the continuity of political thought. It was only gradually, during the Tudor period, that the idea of sovereignty rose to prominence. Even then, it was not yet the concept of a single agent, such as the monarch, endowed with absolute authority, but rather the sovereignty of the "King in Parliament." The actions of the king and the representatives of the people, jointly, were allowed to be sovereign in the name of the law of reason. This sovereignty of the "King in Parliament" antedated the struggle for sovereignty on the part of both the king and the Parliament. Once the idea of sovereignty had supplanted medieval concept of a commonwealth, a struggle for power was almost inevitable.

The conflict between the king and the Parliament entered its crucial stage during the reign of James I. It is for this reason that the bulk of this essay is devoted to his reign. By 1628, when Parliament presented the Petition of Right to Charles I, the major postulates of the struggle had been formulated. A study concerned with the evolution of ideas cannot remain within fixed chronological limits; nevertheless, the end of the second decade of the seventeenth century seemed, in general, a fitting terminal point for this essay. By that time the assimilation of the idea of sovereignty, toward which English constitutional and political thought had tended ever since the Tudor period, can be sufficiently demonstrated.

Because this is a study primarily concerned with the legal ideas which underlay this conflict, it has seemed best to proceed at times by example. Through the thought of men like Sir John Fortescue, Sir Walter Raleigh, James I, and others, we can best grasp the nature and the evolution of the conflict out of which

[4] Albertus Warren, *Eight Reasons Categorical etc.* (London, 1653), p. 5.

the idea of sovereignty emerged victorious. The actual story of the conflict between king and Parliament has been told many times. However, in the case of Parliament, where we are dealing with a corporate body of men, rather than with outstanding individuals, it has seemed well to remain close to the chronological development. Here, too, it has seemed best to show some of the practical motivations which drove members of Parliament on to the quest for sovereignty. It is important to remember that practical considerations set the pace of the conflict, driving both the king, and especially Parliament, forward in their quests for power. And as the struggle continued, liberty became something permissive, a privilege rather than a right.

The idea of absolute sovereignty, then, meant an end to the medieval ideal of liberty as freedom from arbitrary power; private personal property and customary rights could now be taken without appeal. Medieval man, by and large, thought of liberty in terms of property rights; but it is important to realize that the term "property" implied more than just the concept of "private property" which is current in our day. A man could have property rights not only in his land but also in his office if this were hallowed by custom, or in such rights as had accrued to him by prescription through the ages. In this way the rights of individuals were hallowed by tradition which in turn was a vital ingredient of both the common law and the law of nature. To be sure, by modern standards, this concept of liberty seems highly restrictive; we believe that rights should be universal, rather than handed down through custom and tradition. This fact, however, should not blind us to the significance of the controversy about the nature of sovereignty. The principle of individual rights as contrasted with privileges granted by authority is still at issue in our modern world. The crucial seventeenth-century English struggle for sovereignty can show us, at least, how individual freedom became ever more permissive and, more urgently than ever before, raised the question of the role of the individual in the sovereign state.

I

THE TUDOR TRADITION

†

THE SIXTEENTH CENTURY witnessed the gradual disintegration of the medieval concept of the state, for it was during the Tudor period that the sovereignty of the "King in Parliament" emerged, while the law of reason challenged the law of nature as the higher law. Sir John Fortescue, the great Lancastrian lawyer and Chief Justice, gave us his analysis of the constitution before the dawn of the Tudor era. If we compare his writings with those of Elizabethan writers, we will gain some understanding of the changes which the intervening century of Tudor rule had wrought in the thinking of Englishmen about their government.

Lancastrian political thought was, on the whole, medieval and monarchical in tone, and Fortescue, as Chief Justice, upheld the position which was common to his day. No commonwealth could exist, for him, without a king as the head. However, it is important to remember that the idea of the people as the actuating power in government was likewise a vital part of the medieval tradition. For this reason Fortescue could write that polity in the Greek tongue was identical with plurality, which means a government administered by many. "Manage therefore," he exhorted the king, "the commonwealth of thy realm by the counsels of many." [1] As late as 1610, a member of Parliament gave perfect expression to this idea: the "regal power from God, but the actuating thereof is from the people." [2] This designation of functions, with its division of power, was a crucial problem in Lancastrian political thought. What, for Fortescue, then separated the actuating from the regal power?

In answering this question Fortescue dwelt on his theory of the origin of the state. The state, he said, arose from a free compact among the people. The people had originally entered into society in order to enjoy more securely their pristine and inalienable rights, and, this being the purpose of the state, these pristine and inalienable rights were outside the reach of arbitrary might. It was consequently the king's duty to protect the rights and property of his subjects, ". . . and [the king] has no just claim to any power but this." [3] So Fortescue, echoing St. Thomas Aquinas, stated that "the kingdom is not made for the king, but the king for the kingdom." [4]

The line of demarcation which separated the rights of the king (who was protector of the people) from the rights of the subjects (who were protected) was formed by the precedents of common law and the ancient customs of the realm. This was England's bulwark against absolutism. Fortescue looked across the channel, where Frenchmen lived with no such bulwark operating to protect them, where the French king "rules his people by such law as he makes himself," and found the comparison much in England's favor. [5]

The king, then, might not tamper with his subjects' laws and

[1] Sir John Fortescue, *De Natura Legis Naturae* (hereafter *D. N. L.*), in *Works of Sir John Fortescue*, ed. Thomas (Fortescue), Lord Clermont (London, 1869), I, 214.

[2] *Parliamentary Debates*, 1610, ed. S. R. Gardiner (Camden Society, 1862), p. 76.

[3] Sir John Fortescue, *De Laudibus Legum Angliae*, ed. A. Amos (London: J. Butterworth and Son, 1825), p. 38.

[4] Fortescue, *D. N. L.*, p. 253.

[5] Sir John Fortescue, *Governance of England*, ed. Charles Plummer (Oxford: Oxford University Press, 1885), p. 109.

customs: here was the fundamental concept of limited monarchy. Even in that sphere of government and protection which was the king's legitimate function, the rights of the people had continually to be respected and safeguarded. This is well illustrated by the king's pardoning and dispensing powers. The king could, wrote Fortescue, mitigate and remit all punishment, provided he did so without danger to his subjects and without infringing upon the customs and statutes of the realm.[6] The king's pardoning power was thus strictly limited. So was his dispensing power. Said the Chief Justice: if someone ought to repair a bridge, and the king dispense him of that duty, this was of no avail except so far as this dispensation concerned the fine which the king would have taken himself. He could not dispense with the fine which the delinquent owed to the community.[7] The king, then, might dispose of his own rights, but he could not tamper with those of his subjects.

Was there, then, any sphere of government in which Fortescue found the king to be supreme? All matters which were not contrary to the statutes and customs of the realm were to be in his hands.[8] This might be said to include such matters as the powers over peace and war and the appointment of magistrates. It was only in times of war and rebellion that Fortescue conceded to the king truly absolute powers.[9] Yet even here Fortescue would limit the king, for he would join to the king a council partly removed from his immediate control. This council was to concern itself with all matters pertaining to the policy of the realm.[10] The jurisdiction over the royal domain Fortescue would put into the hands of Parliament. The inabil-

[6] Fortescue, *D. N. L.*, p. 214.

[7] Year Book of Henry VI, 37th Year, I, 94-95.

[8] Fortescue, *D. N. L.*, p. 214.

[9] *Ibid.*, p. 215.

[10] Fortescue, *Governance of England*, p. 143, pp. 145 ff. Chrimes holds that these proposals were in no sense constitutional in character. S. B. Chrimes, *English Constitutional Ideas in the Fifteenth Century* (Cambridge: Cambridge University Press, 1936), p. 331. The king's ability to change the council only by the "more part" of the members' consent seems to be, however, a decided limitation on the crown (*Governance of England*, p. 148), this in spite of the fact that the king could probably appoint the original members.

ity of the king to alienate the domain was in the nature of an endowment, enhancing the king's prerogative by enabling him to live on his own.[11] There were good contemporaneous reasons for these further limitations on the king's powers, for the latter half of the fifteenth century had been rent by civil strife and the intrigues of royal minorities. These limitations were meant actually to increase the prestige of the office of kingship.

The king was thus hedged about with limitations. Was he also to be controlled by positive sanctions? Here again, Fortescue was influenced by the events of his time. Fortescue lived shortly after the schism, which had rent the Church in the previous century, had been healed in the Council of Constance. A single Pope reigned where there had been two, and even three, claimants for the throne of St. Peter. Following upon the Council of Constance there had been an increase of papal power, and this may have influenced Sir John Fortescue. While the punishment of a king who governs arbitrarily lay in heaven in the last resort, yet the Pope might have the temporal authority, as the Lord's Vicar on earth, to punish tyrannical monarchs.[12] Thus the theory of papal omnicompetence found an echo in the writings of the English Chief Justice. This is one part of his writings conspicuously absent from quotations by the parliamentary leaders of the seventeenth century.

Although he was not actually controlled by his own subjects, the king, to Fortescue, was limited by the rights of the people as guaranteed through the common law and the customs of the realm. Was it then a static commonwealth which Fortescue envisaged? What if the customs and laws of the commonwealth needed to be adjusted to new conditions? The answer to this question was simple: since these laws and customs were the safeguard of the people, only the people themselves could change them; more precisely, the people themselves must consent to have them reformed, changed, or abrogated. This was

[11] Fortescue, *Governance of England*, p. 155.

[12] Fortescue, *D. N. L.*, p. 263. See George L. Mosse, "Sir John Fortescue and the Problem of Papal Power," *Medievalia et Humanistica*, VII (1950) in press.

the underlying concept of the organization and function of the High Court of Parliament.

If there are inconvenient laws, said Fortescue, they may be reformed, abolished, and amended in Parliament.[13] Statutes are enacted with the "concurrent assent" of the whole kingdom; once so enacted, acts may be only repealed or amended, and that in the same manner in which they were first enacted into law. We have here the constitutional principle that one act of Parliament can only be repealed by another.[14] Once the bill became the law of the land it had to be respected by all.

Fortescue's respect for the authority of Parliament is well illustrated by one of his decisions as Chief Justice. A bill had passed Parliament in an irregular manner. The king had, however, certified by writ that the bill had been properly confirmed by act of Parliament. "This is an act of Parliament," judged Fortescue, "and we wish to be well advised before we annul any act made in Parliament." Judges, Fortescue held, must never render any judgment against the law of the land, even if the king should command them to do so.[15]

That the king was limited by acts of Parliament was natural, for such acts made with the concurrent consent of the people were changes in the binding concepts of the constitution which guaranteed their rights. On the other hand, the king was a vital part of the process, and the words which Fortescue used were, significantly, "concurrent consent," not "absolute power." The king could not make any changes without the consent of the body politic, and the body could not change the foundation of the constitution without the head. England, in short, was a *dominium politicum et regale, politicum* in as much as the concurrent consent of the people was necessary for the enactment of law, *regale* in as much as the king, with this consent, might

[13] Fortescue, *De Laudibus Legem Angliae* (1825), p. 204.

[14] *Ibid.*, p. 56. See also Roger B. Merriman, "Control by National Assemblies of the Repeal of Legislation," *Mélanges d'histoire offerts à M. Charles Bémont* (Paris: Alcan, 1913), pp. 437 ff.

[15] *Year Book of Henry VI*, 33d Year, I, 49; Fortescue, *D. N. L.*, p. 205.

change the laws of the land. And, without his permission, nothing could be enacted by Parliament.

Fortescue's commonwealth was therefore in the medieval tradition. There was here no theory of arbitrary might. The subject was endowed with certain concrete rights which no superior power could take away or change without his consent. As we have seen, these rights were enshrined in the laws and customs of the realm. But these laws and customs, and the rights which they protected, did not stand alone on their own merits. They were in turn protected by the superior law, the law of nature, which sanctified Fortescue's commonwealth, removed it from any merely human power. The people's rights and properties were protected by this superior law because property had been a part of the law of nature long before nations were established. Indeed, as we saw, the secure enjoyment of this property was for him the essence of the founding of the commonwealth.[16] Sanctity of private rights and property was based on both the natural law and the original purpose of the state, and parliamentary statutes must be in conformity with this higher law.

A rule of law was simply the elucidation of the higher law of nature, so that it was, for example, by appealing to the law of nature itself that Fortescue tried to settle the dispute between the houses of Lancaster and York. The authority of parliamentary statutes was therefore not so important as were those principles of natural law from which those statutes were in the first instance derived.[17] Law, even if enacted in Parliament, was never entirely new; in a sense it was only declaratory of the law of nature.

It is evident that no absolute power was possible on the part

[16] Fortescue, *D. N. L.*, pp. 211, 291. It should be noted that while the natural law protected property, the origins of property itself were to be found in man's original sin. Edgar W. Lacy, "The Relation of Property and Dominion to the Law of Nature," *Speculum*, XXIV (July, 1949), pp. 407-409. This is, of course, very similar to John Locke's views on property. See *Two Treatises on Civil Government etc.* (London: 1690), Vol. V (on property).

[17] E. F. Jacob, "Sir John Fortescue and the Law of Nature," *John Ryland's Library Bulletin*, XVIII (July, 1934), 376.

of Parliament, just as it was excluded so far as the king was concerned. So long as there was a law of nature to guarantee the subjects' rights through law, there could be no arbitrary power in any part of the commonwealth.

It would not be too much to say that the weakening of this concept of natural law made possible to a large extent the competition for sovereignty among the different parts of the constitution which was ultimately to be resolved only on the field of battle. This weakening of the power of the law of nature as a guarantee and protection for the ancient laws and customs of England took place, for the most part, during Tudor times. Henry VIII and his Parliaments dissolved the monasteries, and passed the Statute of Uses which transferred possession from the owner of land to him who had the use of it. These were momentous infractions of the ancient right of property. As late as 1550, and, as we hope to show, even later, the judges were still hard put to justify the transfer from one person to another of land which was entailed by the Statute of Uses.[18]

These interventions in the rights of the subject redounded not to the enhancement of the power of the king, but instead to the growing sovereignty of the King in Parliament. It was the growing power of the King in Parliament which constituted the chief element of change in the constitution during Tudor times.

In Christopher St. Germain's *Doctor and Student*, written during the momentous changes in Henry VIII's reign, we already move a step away from Sir John Fortescue's polity. English lawyers, St. Germain tells us, speak of reason where continental lawyers speak of the law of nature.[19] But was St. Germain's law of reason a continuation or a negation of Fortescue's natural law?

This law of reason stated that it was lawful for any man to

[18] Edward T. Lampson, "Some New Light on the Growth of Parliamentary Sovereignty: Wimbish v. Talebois," *American Political Science Review,* XXXV (October, 1941), 952-960. See also C. H. McIlwain, *Constitutionalism, Ancient and Modern* (Ithaca: Cornell University Press, 1947), Appendix.

[19] Christopher St. Germain, *Doctor and Student etc.,* ed. W. Muchall (Cincinnati: Robert Clarke & Co., 1874), p. 12.

defend himself and his goods against unlawful power; [20] but the power of Parliament was a lawful power, and the voice of Parliament was apparently always in tune with the law of reason. "It cannot be thought that a statute that is made by the authority of the whole realm . . . will recite a thing against the truth." [21] Again, no man would think that Parliaments would do "anything that they had not the power to do." [22] St. Germain's law of reason justified, and did not restrain, the transference of a man's property or the taking away of a man's goods. It justified the dissolution of the monasteries and confirmed the legality of the Statute of Uses. Here surely we have an early stage in the waning influence of the property-protecting law of nature of Sir John Fortescue. It seems as if the law of nature and the law of reason were not identical, as St. Germain would have us believe.

This is made still clearer if we glance at the *Reading of the Statute of Westminster the First*, written by James Morice in 1578, forty-seven years after the publication of St. Germain's *Doctor and Student*. Morice, like Fortescue, traced the origin of the best kind of monarch to the common assent of the people,

wherein the princes (not by licentious will but by law, that is by the prudent precepts of reason agreed upon and made the covenant of the commonwealth) may justly govern and command, and the people in due obedience safely live and quietly enjoy their own.[23]

Law was in this way equivalent to the prudent precepts of reason agreed upon so that the people, free from arbitrary power,

[20] *Ibid.*, p. 7.

[21] *Ibid.*, p. 297.

[22] *Ibid.*, p. 303. A still more sweeping assertion of parliamentary power is found in St. Germain's "Spirituality and Temporality," *The Apology of Sir Thomas Moore etc.*, ed. A. I. Taft (London: Oxford University Press, 1930), p. 228. It seems, therefore, not entirely true to say, as F. L. Baumer does, that St. Germain protected property in the same measure as Sir John Fortescue. *The Early Tudor Theory of Kingship* (New Haven: Yale University Press, 1940), p. 134.

[23] James Morice, "Readings on the Statute of Westminster the First" (hereafter "Readings"), ed. T. Lampson (doctoral dissertation, Harvard University, 1934), p. 7.

might enjoy their own. Were these precepts of reason, an integral part of Morice's state, equivalent to the law of nature?

There are two passages in Morice which will throw more light on this idea of reason in relation to Fortescue's law of nature. "To make laws for the good of the people . . . ever have been in all civil policies . . . appertaining to such as have sovereign rule and possess chief authority in the realm. . . ." [24] But what did Morice mean by "sovereign rule"? Did he, as Fortescue would have done, exempt property from the control of the sovereign power in the name of the natural law (or the precepts of reason) on which the commonwealth was founded? "By grave and wise council, advice and concert of his whole realm, the King only has authority to make new laws or ordinances touching the life, lands, goods or inheritances of the subjects. . . ." [25] The sovereign power was the King in Parliament, and in this capacity no right of the subject seems to be removed from his law-making power. Morice's precepts of reason had little or nothing in common with Fortescue's medieval law of nature.

Both St. Germain's and Morice's emphasis on Parliament as representative of the whole realm merits consideration. Steadily the idea seems to have gained ground that the people might dispose of their own rights, though the king alone could not do it. We will see echoes of this belief in both Sir Thomas Smith, writing some ten years before Morice's treatise, and Richard Hooker, composing his *Ecclesiastical Polity* even while Morice was giving his readings. We seem to be traveling the path toward Parliament's assertion in the Apology of 1604 that "The voice of the people in things of their knowledge is said to be as the voice of God."

Richard Hooker may serve to illustrate the blend of the old tradition with the mounting idea of parliamentary power. Yet even here the new was more in evidence than was the old. To Hooker, as to Fortescue, the power of the ruler must come either from God, by immediate appointment, or, more fre-

[24] James Morice, "Readings," p. 23.
[25] *Ibid.*, p. 25.

quently, from the consent of the people.[26] Though royal government was not necessarily the only kind of government instituted by God, once kings have been exalted to their royal estate they may exact all lawful obedience.[27] The emphasis here was on the "lawful," for the king was strictly limited in his functions. As in Fortescue, the people yielded to government in order to have rest, tranquillity, and protection.[28] Here, too, the king had the power over peace and war.[29]

The king could not touch the people's rights protected by law. "Laws therefore," Hooker wrote, "they are not therefore which public approbation has not made so." [30] Of that public approbation the king was a vital part. "The Parliament of England . . . is that whereupon the very essence of all government within the kingdom does depend . . . it consisteth of the king, and of all that within the land are subject unto him. . . ." [31] England was, at least on the face of it, still a *dominium politicum et regale:* the king was limited, but he was not controlled, and he must be left to divine revenge.[32] "Wherefore, since the Kings of England are within their own dominions the most high, and can have no peer, how is it possible that any either civil or ecclesiastical person under them should have over them coercive power, when such power would make that person so far forth his superiors superior ruler and judge." [33] So much for Fortescue's Lord's Vicar on earth, or for John Calvin's "elect."

Hooker, too, believed in the existence of a higher body of

[26] Richard Hooker, *Of the Laws of Ecclesiastical Polity* (hereafter *Polity*), VIII, 176. Two editions of this work have been used: the Everyman's Library edition (London: J.M.Dent and Co., [Vol.I, 1925; Vol.II, 1922]) and the R.A. Houk edition (New York: Columbia University Press, 1931). The Houk edition is of the eighth book only, and subsequent reference to the eighth book will signify this edition. Kings by conquest were only bound by the laws of God and nature, but "the most sweet form of kingly government" was that instituted by agreement of the king and people. *Ibid,* 176, 177.

[27] *Ibid.,* p. 172.

[28] *Ibid.*

[29] *Ibid.,* VIII, 182.

[30] *Ibid.,* I, 194.

[31] *Ibid.,* VIII, 241.

[32] *Ibid.,* p. 285.

[33] *Ibid.,* p. 291.

law. He seemed to stress the natural and divine law in the medieval manner. The highest law was the law of God; it was any universal rule or canon by which human actions are framed.[34] The first outward manifestation of this eternal law was the law of nature. It was this law which ordered all natural processes, the heavens, and the elements in all the world.[35] But the natural law as such governed only nature itself. It was the law of reason which bound man, the reasonable creature in the world. By using their own reason men might perceive the law of reason, God's order for man.[36]

There is an apparently strong similarity between Hooker's law of reason and the old medieval natural law. A human law must conform to the law of reason. To Fortescue, as we have seen, human law was also merely a clarification of the law of nature. The crucial question, then, is what were the contents of Hooker's law of reason? Did it, like the law of nature of old, remove the rights of the people from all human interference?

Hooker's law of reason lacked the concrete precepts of Fortescue's law of nature. The Scriptures were contained in this law of reason, and human laws must not contradict the Scriptures.[37] This, at least, was the negative content of the law of reason. Its positive content was the instructions which natural reason gave each man to know and distinguish good from evil and virtue from vice.[38] This may seem vague, but to Hooker every man was born with the light of reason,[39] and it was easy therefore for common sense to discern the good. Yet human laws were necessary to serve as the guide posts of human actions.

Clearly Hooker's law of reason was extremely broad in content; it did not descend, seemingly, to particulars regarding the actual governing of the state. It is apparent that under Hooker's universal law no one could steal or take away a person's goods

---

[34] *Ibid.*, I, 150, 152.
[35] *Ibid.*, pp. 155 ff.
[36] *Ibid.*, pp. 154-155.
[37] *Ibid.*, III, 326.
[38] *Ibid.*, I, 182.
[39] *Ibid.*, p. 176.

and life.[40] But could the commonwealth do that which private persons could not? The very essence of the government of England, as we saw, was Parliament, and Parliament consisted of the king and his subjects.

The public power of all societies is above every soul contained in the same societies. And the principal use of that power is to give laws unto all that are under it; which laws in such cases we must obey, unless there be reason showed which may necessarily enforce that the Law of Reason or of God enjoin the contrary.[41]

The common good was above the individual. Hooker thought that to change laws was a dangerous thing, but when the laws were inimical to the good of the community—for example, directed against the good for which human societies were instituted—they should be changed.[42] It is clear that the community as embodied in Parliament was the supreme lawgiver, and that Parliament had the power to make laws ". . . for all persons in all causes. . . ." [43] Would it be reasonable to assume, then, that property was here included? There may be a hint of the answer in Hooker's description of what is "good" so far as the law of reason is concerned. Of divers good things, one might be principal and pre-eminent. To retain one's possession was without sin, yet as a principal and overriding good Hooker cited those who sold their possessions and laid them at the feet of the apostles.[44] Here public good overrode the private rights of property.

If the public good was so far ahead of the private, Parliament, the embodiment of the community, could make laws for all persons in the name of the common good. The law of reason seemed to have no precept to the contrary.

[40] *Ibid.*, pp. 180-181.
[41] *Ibid.*, p. 228.
[42] *Ibid.*, IV, 422.
[43] *Ibid.*, VIII, 248.
[44] *Ibid.*, II, 181. Indeed Hooker goes so far as to state: ". . . in matter of state the weight many times of some one man's authority is thought reason sufficient, even to sway over whole nations." *Ibid.*, I, 265.

In the last resort Hooker had more in common with the new ways of St. Germain than he had with the old ways of Sir John Fortescue. One has the feeling that Hooker was torn by conflicting emotions. On the one hand, as the zealous Anglican, he set out to prove to the Puritans that they too were bound by the decisions of a Parliament representing the community. And so he had to exalt the power of Parliament, to emancipate it from the property-protecting bonds of the medieval natural law. In the end we find a doctrine not too far removed from the idea of reason of state, which was to be, as we shall see, more than a mere royal doctrine. On the other hand, Hooker believed almost passionately in the law as the cohesive element in the commonwealth. The king must hold his power under the law.[45]

Of law there can be no less acknowledged, than that her seat is the bosom of God, her voice the harmony of the world: all things in heaven and earth do her homage, the very least as feeling her care, and the greatest as not exempted from her power: both Angels and men and creatures of what condition soever, though each in different sort and manner, yet all with uniform consent, admiring her as the mother of their peace and joy.[46]

The seat of the law of reason may have been in the bosom of God, but the rights and properties of the people were enshrined in the more mundane bosom of the community as represented in Parliament. Hooker was, after all, a man reared in the Tudor tradition.

We have traced the weakening power of the natural law through three different writers of the Tudor period. In all of them this weakening of the medieval concept of law redounded not to the benefit of the king, who was still limited by law, but to the enhanced power of the King in Parliament as representative of the community as a whole.

It was Queen Elizabeth's Secretary of State, Sir Thomas Smith, who typified most clearly for our purposes the changes which a hundred years of Tudor rule had wrought in the con-

---

[45] *Ibid.*, VIII, 169.
[46] *Ibid.*, I, 232.

stitution. With him, too, the king was limited by the law. A commonwealth was

> ... a society or common doing of a multitude of free men collected together and united by common accord and covenants amongst themselves for the conservation of themselves as well in peace as in war.[47]

Here we are in the tradition of Sir John Fortescue, for he too had believed that the state had its origin in a free compact among the people. Moreover, to Smith, too, the law of the land was the ligament which held together the constitution and defined the spheres of influence of king and people. The king, according to Smith, becomes a tyrant if he "breaketh laws already made at his pleasure, maketh other without the advice and consent of the people." [48] The king's power must give way when it comes into conflict with the rights of the subject. The king might dispense with his own rights but not with those of his subjects. In popular actions, where part of the fine went to the declarator and part to the prince, the prince could dispense only with his part. In criminal actions the king could give pardon only if the plaintiff prove unwilling to take up renewed accusation against the convicted criminal.[49] On the other hand, the king had the absolute power to appoint all magistrates and the power to control foreign policy. He was therefore also supreme in times of war.[50]

The king was limited. But the problem of how to control the monarch and prevent him from overstepping his functions was

---

[47] Sir Thomas Smith, *De Republica Anglorum* (hereafter *Republica*), ed. L. Alston (Cambridge: Cambridge University Press, 1906), p. 20. For a more detailed comparison of Fortescue and Smith, see G. L. Mosse, "Change and Continuity in the Tudor Constitution," *Speculum*, XXII (1947), 18-28.

[48] *Ibid.*, p. 15.

[49] *Ibid.*, p. 61.

[50] *Ibid.*, p. 63. However, Smith recommends punishment through the laws of the land in times of rebellion and he would deny to the king absolute powers in such an emergency: *Republica*, p. 59. Here Fortescue, living in times when rebellion was an all too frequent occurrence, would extend the king's absolute powers to rebellions as well as war. *D. N. L.*, p. 215. Part of the answer to the difference between the two men can be found in the tightening of the treason laws during Tudor times.

not solved by Sir Thomas Smith. Queen Elizabeth's Secretary of State side-stepped this issue. If the king became a tyrant, the "learned" would judge as to the best way out of the dilemma, but to meddle with laws and government was a dangerous thing.[51] With Smith, as with the other writers we have discussed, it was the law which limited the king. Smith's awareness of the importance of the common law is somewhat surprising when we remember that he was originally trained in the continental *ius civile*. One might, therefore, have expected him to voice the sentiments of Padua rather than those of the Inns of Court. When his actual conversion to the principles of the common law took place is difficult to determine, but even in his inaugural lecture as Professor of Civil Law at Cambridge there were some discordant notes. The technicalities of the civil law were derided while the eloquence and vigor not infrequently exhibited in common law courts were praised.[52]

But it may not be forgotten that in the minds of many men, even during the constitutional struggles of the next century, as we hope to show, the two bodies of law were by no means deadly enemies. Fortescue himself found words of praise for the civil law,[53] and Smith seemed indeed to have thought of the common law in civilian terms: "That our law," he told the people of France, "which is called of us the common law, as ye would say *Ius Civile*." [54]

On the face of it, Smith followed Fortescue in determining the place of Parliament in the constitution. The king, of course, could not change the laws which protected the people's rights without the aid of the people's representatives assembled in Parliament. These representatives were present in order to "advertise, consult and show" what was good and necessary for the commonwealth.[55] The king, here, was a vital part of Parlia-

---

[51] Smith, *Republica*, p. 13.

[52] J. B. Mullinger, *The University of Cambridge etc.* (Cambridge: Cambridge University Press, 1884), II, 129, 132.

[53] "Those illustrious Civil Laws, which have so long born, as it were, the care of all the world." Fortescue, *D. N. L.*, p. 225.

[54] Smith, *Republica*, p. 70-71.

[55] *Ibid.*, p. 48.

ment: those bills of which he disapproved were "utterly dashed and of no effect." "To be short, the Prince is the life, the head, and the authority of all things that be done in the realm of England." [56] That which was done in Parliament was "called firm and stable and sanctum, and is taken for law." [57] With these sentiments Sir John Fortescue would have been in hearty agreement. For both Fortescue and Smith, Parliament was primarily the "High Court" of the realm. Fortescue discussed the reforming and abolishing of laws in connection with delays which might at any time arise in pleading; for Smith, bills were merely a matter of giving judgment in Parliament.[58]

Yet Smith, even better than Hooker or Morice, illustrates the changes of constitutional progress. Sir Thomas Smith did not even mention the law of reason. He was no longer bound by the fetters of any superior law. In consequence, Parliament actually "abrogateth old laws and maketh new," and it could also change the rights and possessions of private men, for all were represented in Parliament.[59] Here there is no question, as there had been with Hooker, of whether the law of reason, however broad in content, might not restrain a Parliament that was making laws for all persons and all causes.

Without referring to superior and restraining laws, Smith listed the powers of Parliament, a list solidly grounded in Tudor

---

[56] *Ibid.,* p. 58, 62.

[57] *Ibid.,* p. 49.

[58] Fortescue, *De Laudibus Legum Angliae,* p. 204. Smith, *Republica,* p. 64.

[59] *Ibid.,* p. 49. Here are found all the enumerations of parliamentary powers. For a criticism of this view see Margaret A. Judson, *The Crisis of the Constitution* (New Brunswick: Rutgers University Press, 1949), p. 84 (n. 43). It is quite true that Smith used the word "change" rather than "abrogate, abolish, or dispose" when dealing with Parliament's power over property. Yet we shall see when discussing cases concerning uses in the Elizabethan courts that here a more sweeping language was used. It is undoubtedly true that the legislative sovereignty of Parliament was by no means consciously established or a fact in late Tudor times, as Arthur von Mehren points out: "The Judicial Conception of Legislation in Tudor England," *Interpretations of Modern Legal Philosophies,* ed. Paul Sayre (New York: Oxford University Press, 1947), pp. 760–763. It is with the growth of this idea that we are here, in part, concerned and Smith is the start only of such a development.

precedent. Parliament could change religion, as it had done several times in Smith's lifetime, it could regulate the succession, as it had done under Henry VIII, and it actually disposed of the rights and possessions of private men by transferring land when Smith was as yet a youth. Indeed, Smith had been a member of Parliament during the reign of Queen Mary, and he had seen the queen frequently going out of her way to placate a House of Commons which in 1555 rejected outright a measure against the exiled Protestants.[60]

Here, then, we find in the constitution a pure reflection of the growing ascendancy of Parliament. Once again its power was based partly on the assertion that the community was represented in Parliament. Parliament was "absolute," though no doubt to Smith only in a legal sense, meaning without appeal.[61] But it was absolute enough to make new laws and to change the people's rights and properties. Smith as well as Hooker, Morice, and St. Germain no longer excepted certain rights from the lawmaking power of the state on the grounds of natural law.

Professor Julius Hatschek has placed Smith as the transmitter of the idea of sovereignty into England.[62] It is important to point out, however, that the idea of the commonwealth as presented by Sir John Fortescue had begun to weaken in England even before the continental development of a theory of sovereignty got under way. St. Germain wrote when Jean Bodin, the French political writer who gave us the classic definition of sovereignty, was still a mere youth. Smith, though a contemporary of Bodin, reflected the actual events of Tudor times. Hooker in turn was concerned with a specifically English problem: to lead the Puritans back into the Anglican fold. It was a task, however, not entirely unrelated to the issue con-

---

[60] Wallace Notestein, *The Winning of the Initiative by the House of Commons* (London: Oxford University Press, 1924), pp. 14 (n. 1), 15.

[61] Smith, *Republica*, XXXII. "Absolute," Dr. Alston holds, means "without appeal" in the judicial sense. This is in tune with Smith's analysis of the constitution in legal terms.

[62] Julius Hatschek, *Englisches Staatsrecht* (Tuebingen: J. C. B. Mohr, 1905), I, 611.

fronting France at the same time, to assert the superiority of the state over all kinds of religious schism.

The fact remains that during the century following Fortescue's death the idea of complete sovereignty developed in England itself. When a member of Parliament cried out in 1621, "We sit here as our ancestors did to *make* laws," [63] he showed a felt need for change of the medieval tradition. But even as early as 1584 the Lord Treasurer could state as commonplace "that of the three estates doth consist the whole body of the Parliament able to *make* laws." [64] When Sergeant Heylen asserted in Parliament, in Elizabeth's reign, that the queen had power over everyone's property, "all the house hemmed, and laughed and talked. . . ." [65] Would they have behaved in a similar manner if Heylen had asserted the right of the queen in Parliament to dispose of every Englishman's property? The exclamation of a member of Parliament during the debates of 1610 might well sum up the development which we have been discussing. "The King of England [is] the most absolute King in his Parliament, but, of himself, his Power is limited by Law." [66]

Yet we must keep the continuity of the medieval tradition in mind along with the change. The king was still limited by the law which assigned to him his place in the constitution. Government and the protection of the state were his sphere. The laws were the sinews of the state which divided the rights of king and people, and they could only be changed with the consent of the people assembled in Parliament. However, the waning power of natural law robbed the law of England of one of its main supports. The highest court of the realm was becoming "absolute," the seat of the people's rights was being transferred from the bosom of God to the High Court of Parliament.

---

[63] Alford, typically enough a leader of the parliamentary opposition to the king. *Commons Debates, 1621*, ed. Notestein, Relf, Simpson (New Haven: Yale University Press, 1935), II, 120. (Italics mine.)

[64] Sir Simon D'Ewes, *Journals of All the Parliaments etc.* (London: 1804), p. 350. (Italics mine.)

[65] *Ibid.*, p. 633.

[66] *Parliamentary Debates, 1610*, p. 89.

A struggle for power was bound to ensue between the two members of the commonwealth, the king and the Parliament, each making a bid for "absolute" authority. The defenders of the common law, on the other hand, with Coke to guide them, tried to take their stand on medieval precedent. They talked about the law of reason, attempted to make it once again a more concrete law than the general precepts of a Hooker or a Morice.

The problem thus becomes one of sovereignty. The examination of this question requires a brief discussion of the idea of sovereignty itself, as it was being elaborated in France under the stress of religious war, for though England itself was moving toward sovereignty, yet there was undoubtedly French influence on English constitutional thought. It was in France that the idea of sovereignty was elaborated and made explicit in its classical form.

II

THE IDEA OF SOVEREIGNTY

†

THE FRENCH THEORIST JEAN BODIN published his tract, the *Methodus*, in 1566, the year after Sir Thomas Smith wrote his *Republica*. Bodin's *République* appeared more than a decade later. He was thus elaborating his ideas in France at the same time that Smith, Morice, and Hooker were arguing along similar lines in England.

"La République est un droit gouvernement de plusieurs menages de ce que leur est commune avec puissance souveraine." [1] The two key words in Bodin's definition of sovereignty would seem to be *droit* and *souveraine*. By sovereignty he understood the "puissance absolue et perpetuelle d'une République." [2] Sovereignty must be a perpetual power; the ruler could not be truly sovereign if he were but a trustee of the people and if the people could at any time revoke the power which they had conferred upon him. The sovereign must be absolute, and must not be subject to the command of any of his subordinates. He alone must be able to give laws to his people,

[1] Jean Bodin, *La République etc.* (Paris: 1576), p. 4.
[2] *Ibid.*, p. 93.

make new ones, and abrogate the old.[3] The sovereign was the highest power.

What were the chief marks of his sovereignty? How could an outsider judge who was sovereign in a nation? Bodin's concept of sovereignty seems to have evolved partly out of his interest in comparing the diverse governments of Europe,[4] for he was vitally interested in applying his definition of sovereignty to the nations of his day. The first mark of sovereignty was the sovereign's power as a lawgiver, and all other signs of sovereignty were included under this, the supreme mark of power. The power over foreign relations, the appointment of magistrates, the pardoning power, the right of coinage, and the right to collect taxes were subordinate, but essential, privileges inherent in the sovereign power.[5]

Here seems to be a picture of the true despot, a ruler completely above the power of the people. It hardly seems necessary to point out that even if the prince became a tyrant, the subject could not touch him.[6] Might seems to make right, and the word *droit* in Bodin's original definition seems devoid of meaning. And yet Bodin wrote in the tradition of Fortescue, for the sovereign, absolute though he might be, was still encompassed and limited by the laws of God and of nature.[7] Here was the *droit gouvernement*.

To Bodin as to Fortescue, these were very real limitations. Natural law commanded that the subject's goods could not be taken from him without due cause. The ruler must keep faith in any contracts which he might have made with any of his subjects. Moreover, the fundamental laws of the nation, such as the Salic law in France, since they concerned the very founding of the state, were without the king's reach.[8] Bodin quotes with approbation Seneca's dictum: to the king authority over all, to

[3] *Ibid.*, p. 97.

[4] Jean Bodin, *Easy Method for the Comprehension of History*, ed. and tr. B. Reynolds (New York: Columbia University Press, 1945), pp. 178 ff.

[5] Bodin, *La République*, pp. 155, 163, 168, 176, 179.

[6] *Ibid.*, pp. 222, 225.

[7] *Ibid.*, p. 97.

[8] *Ibid.*, pp. 100, 102.

private persons property.[9] We seem to be back with Fortescue. The king was sovereign in all matters which allowed of sovereignty, but property was without the reach of any human interference.

It was in his emphasis on the idea of sovereignty as residing in the lawgiver that Bodin struck a new note. Laws were not merely declaratory of the law of nature; they were in the breath of the ruler so long as they did not conflict with the law of nature itself. Moreover, to Bodin, the good of the community must precede the good of the individual: for the good of the state property might be taken away from the subject. This, too, was a precept of natural law.[10] Here was an argument which could be used to nullify the very limitations which Bodin put upon the sovereign. The idea of "reason of state" was intrinsically opposed to the Frenchman's definition of a ruler who was at once "sovereign" yet also limited.

The evolution of French political thought after Bodin gave rise to an increasing emphasis on the idea of *souveraineté* as against the idea of *droit*.[11] That absolute sovereignty had become a fact in France (so far as actual practice was concerned) at least one English observer concluded only thirteen years after Bodin's death. Henry IV had the entire sovereignty to himself "because he can make the Parliament do what he pleases, or else do what he pleases without them." [12] The President of the Parliament was not bound to judge according to the written law, but according to the equity drawn out of it, "which liberty doth not so much admit Conscience as leave Wit without limit." [13] The French state, then, was "of monarchies the most absolute. Because the king there not only makes peace

---

[9] *Ibid.*, p. 115.

[10] *Ibid.*, pp. 114-115.

[11] William Farr Church, *French Constitutional Thought in the Sixteenth Century* (Cambridge, Mass.: Harvard University Press, 1941), pp. 243 ff.

[12] Sir Thomas Overbury, "Observations on the State of France," *Stuart Tracts*, ed. C. H. Firth (New York: E. P. Dutton and Company, n.d.), p. 223. Another English observer of the French scene noted that the Parliament of Paris was stripped of any real power. Robert Dallington, *A Method for Travel etc.* (London, n.d.).

[13] Overbury, "Observations," p. 225.

and war, calls and dissolves Parliaments, pardoneth, natural-
iseth . . . but even makes laws and imposes taxes at his pleasure." [14]

Sir Thomas Overbury saw the king of France as embodying
the entire sovereignty in himself. But it is equally clear that
Overbury was a little astounded at the extent of the king's
power, for he "even makes law" at his pleasure. Yet, in contrast
to Smith, he believed France to be the greatest united force of
Christendom.[15] English royalist writers were to find it advan-
tageous in their struggle with Parliament to stress the similarities between England and France, both "True Monarchies."

In France, by 1609 the element of sovereignty had replaced
and driven out the element of the *droit*, at least in the eyes of the
visiting Englishman. Yet it must be added that even by 1632 the
tradition of Bodin seems to have been still alive in France. Le
Bret, the chief defender of the monarchy at the time of the
Fronde, still upheld the sanctity of property as well as of contracts on the part of the king, although otherwise the king was
absolute. This seems to have been the usual argument of those
defending the royal power in that crisis.[16] Although the French
jurists regarded the will of the prince as law in all matters pertaining to government, they nevertheless refused to part with
the fundamental conception that there existed a final justice
over and above all men.[17]

It seems, then, that in France, while Louis XIV might say,
"*L'état, c'est moi*," constitutional thinkers never entirely
agreed with this opinion. But there was an increasing emphasis
upon the *souverainté*, though Thomas Hobbes's concept of
absolute sovereignty was not to be a significant factor in French
political thought.[18] In Tudor England, even as Bodin was writing his *République*, the medieval idea of *droit gouvernement*

[14] *Ibid.*, p. 221.

[15] *Ibid.*, p. 225,

[16] Paul Rice Doolin, *The Fronde* (Cambridge, Mass.: Harvard University
Press, 1935), pp. 84-91.

[17] Church, *French Constitutional Thought*, p. 334.

[18] *Ibid.*, p. 335.

was giving way to a more arbitrary definition of political authority; here too we have the gradual adoption of his theory of sovereignty and the gradual discarding of his limitations of natural law. Nevertheless, the development of English constitutional theory in the direction of sovereignty antedates Bodin's systematization of that concept; the *Methodus*, where we only get the first inkling of the doctrine of sovereignty, appeared in the same year as did the *Republica* of Sir Thomas Smith. The *République* itself did not appear until 1576, two years before Morice's *Readings*. Could Bodin have influenced the English development directly? Smith might have met and conversed with Bodin during his sojourn as English ambassador in France before either book had appeared. If that was so, we have no concrete evidence to prove it. The *Methodus* was known in England by 1580 and the *République* was read in Cambridge by 1581.[19] This evidence postdates even Morice's treatise. Bodin visited England in 1581 and admired English institutions. He was received at court, where the learned Dr. John Dee met him and found the meeting important enough to chronicle in his diary.[20] Gabriel Harvey corresponded with Bodin in spite of his dislike for the French lawyer.[21] At last, in 1606, Richard Knolles translated the *République*.[22]

But it hardly needed English translation or adaptations for

[19] Leonard F. Dean, "Bodin's Methodus in England before 1625," *Studies in Philology*, XXXIX (April, 1942), 160-166. The question whether Bodin heard his work read during a visit to the University of Cambridge has been disputed: Henri Baudrillart, *Jean Bodin et Son Temps* (Paris, 1835), p. 128.

[20] *The Private Diary of Dr. John Dee*, ed. J. D. Halliwell (Camden Society, 1842), p. 10. A summary of Bodin's movements in England is given in Summerfield Baldwin, "Jean Bodin and the League," *Catholic Historical Review*, XXIII (July, 1937), 160-184.

[21] *Gabriel Harvey's Marginalia*, ed. G. C. M. Smith (Stratford on Avon: Shakespeare Head Press, 1913), p. 116. In spite of his dislike for "Mr. Bodkin," Harvey had to concede that "you cannot step into a scholar's study but (ten to one) you shall likely find open either Bodin's De Republica or. . . ." p. 79.

[22] Richard Knolles, *The Six Books of a Commonwealth etc.* (London, 1606). Knolles was also the author of a *History of Turkey*. For more detailed analysis of Bodin's influence on specific English writings, see G. L. Mosse, "The Influence of Jean Bodin's République on English Political Thought," *Medievalia et Humanistica*, V (Spring, 1948), pp. 73-83.

Bodin to be read across the channel. Now and then we come across a reference to his name in the constitutional writings of the day which shows that the writer was acquainted with his works. Where there was no direct reference, there was at times good internal evidence to show that Bodin had been read and assimilated. The difficulty in showing direct influence lies chiefly in the fact, mentioned above, that England had outrun France in the development of constitutional thought even by the time Bodin wrote the *République*. Bodin may have been read so widely in England precisely because his ideas fitted in with an already present trend in English constitutional theory. His emphasis upon a superior power located within (rather than without) the state, and his emphasis upon the importance of the public good seem to echo through Smith, Morice, and Hooker. It was Jean Bodin who clearly defined the idea of sovereignty, and his contribution to English constitutional thought was to put his definition at the service of the writers across the channel.

The use which English writers made of Bodin can be illustrated through the thought of three different men, each with his own attitude toward Bodin's ideas. William Fullbeck's writings appeared at the turn of the century. A common lawyer as well as a doctor of civil law, he constantly referred to Jean Bodin. If these references were mostly to Bodin as a chronicler and historian, the contents of Fullbeck's works leave no doubt as to his acquaintance with the *République*.

Law, he said, he intended to interpret as an order established by authority.[23] In the last resort, God was the author of this law. Human law, Fullbeck held, despite individual variations, had certain universal theorems, and these universal theorems were equivalent to "perfect reason." [24] Here we seem to have something roughly equivalent to the law of reason. The prime content of that perfect reason was to Fullbeck that all law must be stable, written, and determined. "God ruleth that Common-

---

[23] William Fullbeck, *Direction or Preparative to the Study of Law* (hereafter *Direction or Preparative*), ed. J. H. Stirling (London, 1829), p. 4.
[24] *Ibid.*, pp. 5, 11.

wealth which is governed by written law," for such law is the guardian and defender of liberty.[25] It, in accordance with the end of all law, rendered equal justice to all, and guaranteed the people's safety.[26]

How far, then, was law an order established by authority? Here Fullbeck seems to be facing a dilemma. Law, he felt, must be written and determined, and yet it depends upon arbitrary authority. In the end, the authority establishing the law seems to have been that of "common assent." [27] Obviously Bodin's ruler as lawgiver did not fit in with Fullbeck's English training. It is very interesting that, unlike Smith, he never mentioned Parliament itself as a giver of laws. Fullbeck was a common lawyer, and he may have had his doubts about Parliament's power over the common law.[28]

It was Fullbeck as common lawyer who wrote,

> Bodinus saith not well, who putteth this difference between a law and a custom, in that a custom is accepted by plausible argument of the multitude, but a law springeth up in a moment, and is commanded by the authority of the ruler, many times against the liking of them that are bound by it . . . for Common Law is that which is made and approved by Common allowance, and therefore it is law, because it is commonly used for law.[29]

The common law was altered by reason rather than by sovereignty, by consent rather than by command.[30] This was not the voice of Sir Thomas Smith. Though Parliament had its place in the realm, it was a position quite distinct from that of the common law. Statutes or acts of Parliament were made by common assembly, but not the common law, which he also termed "common reason." [31] Here we have an all-important

[25] *Ibid.*, pp. 16, 17.
[26] *Ibid.*, p. 4.
[27] William Fullbeck, *The Pandects of the Law of Nations* (hereafter *Pandects*), (London, 1603), p. 92.
[28] *Vide infra*, chap. vii.
[29] Fullbeck, *Pandects*, p. 92.
[30] William Fullbeck, *A Parallele or Conference of the Civil Law, the Canon Law, and the Common Law of this Realm of England* (London, 1601), Preface.
[31] Fullbeck, *Pandects*, p. 105.

division: common law, which was equivalent to perfect reason, and statute law, which came from the king because the king summoned Parliament.[32]

Indeed, Fullbeck did not think much of Parliament's powers. Tribute and subsidies, for example, were lawful, to be levied by the king as a remembrance of the Conquest. This, he said, was true in spite of the fact that the people seemed to offer it rather than that the king commanded it.[33]

Why did Fullbeck not find the highest authority of the realm in the King in Parliament, along with Smith and Morice? As we have seen, common law seemed to him to be the basic law of the realm, in tune with the law of reason, for the king could repeal penal statutes, but he could not touch the common law.[34] Here the law of reason is used as a bar to sovereignty and seems to be identical with the old law of nature. This attempt to give to the law of reason some of the force of the old law of nature would be continued by common lawyers. It opposed the way in which men like Christopher St. Germain and Richard Hooker used this concept of higher law, in order to allow for the inclusion of absolute power within its confines. Fullbeck seemed to give the common law an independent status in the realm, removed from arbitrary authority. He seemed here to have a great deal of common ground with his great contemporary, Sir Edward Coke. But Fullbeck is particularly interesting because of the dilemma which he presented: he accepted the idea that there must be an authority somewhere in the state that can establish law by its will, but found it impossible to reconcile this with the medieval concept of the law as removed from arbitrary authority.

If Fullbeck was necessarily vague on the subject of sovereignty, he was quite explicit as to the nature of the liberties which the common law must protect according to the dictates of perfect reason. "The end of the law is to settle the property

[32] *Ibid.*, p. 105.
[33] *Ibid.*, p. 69.
[34] *Ibid.*, p. 173.

and right things in them to whom they belong." [35] Here Full-beck was both on the solid ground of medieval precedent and in tune with Bodin. What about the king's power? Here, too, Fullbeck confined himself to medieval precedent. Kings were chosen for the protection of the people, and therefore they could not take their subjects' goods without lawful cause.[36] Only in some special instances could goods be taken, as in the cases of felons and of condemned criminals. It is not without irony that Fullbeck added, ". . . if anyone think this prerogative too large for an absolute monarch, he must be so base that he cannot judge such a high estate." [37] The king's goods were out-side the human law just as were those of the subjects. But in conformity with his emphasis upon a written and determined law, such things as accrued to the king as a matter of record could not be taken, even by prescription. On the other hand, if there was no record, a man might prescribe even against the king.[38]

The king was thus decidedly limited. But his real limitation was less from Parliament than from the common law. Benefits and prerogatives were allowed to the king by the law of na-tions, which was equivalent to the common law.[39] For the king had only such pre-eminence over the subject as the common law allowed him, a position similar to that held by Sir William Staunford in his *Exposition of the King's Prerogative*, a book dear to Sir Edward Coke.[40] This prerogative of the king con-sisted in a series of customary rights which could not infringe upon the property and ancient rights of the subject. For Full-beck, furthermore, magistrates as well as the king were limited by the law. Here, as in Fortescue, it was the law which limited the king, a law removed from arbitrary power.

Bodin's idea of sovereignty did not fare well at the hands

[35] *Ibid.*, p. 144.
[36] *Ibid.*, pp. 12-13.
[37] *Ibid.*, pp. 8-9.
[38] *Ibid.*, p. 111.
[39] *Ibid.*, p. 73.
[40] Sir William Staunford, *An Exposition of the King's Prerogative etc.* (London, 1590).

of this common lawyer. True, property was protected by both, but Fullbeck had to divorce the idea of law from the power of a human ruler. Instead of concentrating on sovereignty and minimizing the *droit*, Fullbeck, like Coke, took the opposite road. As for Bodin, said Fullbeck, "I excuse him thus: *nullum fuit magnum ingenium sine mixtura clementia.*" [41] Fullbeck's work derives a particular interest from his recognition and final rejection, in the name of the medieval tradition, of the idea of legislative sovereignty.

Both Sir John Hayward's and Edward Forsett's arguments run closer to Bodin's. Sir John Hayward, Elizabethan historian and publicist, shows a more concrete knowledge of the Frenchman's writings than does his contemporary, Edward Forsett, landowner, justice of the peace, and onetime surveyor in the Office of Works. Indeed, Hayward, in his answer to the prominent Jesuit pamphleteer, Robert Parsons, produced virtually a paraphrase of the *République:* as one God ruled the world, one master the family, so a state should be governed by one commander; the prince was a sovereign who acknowledged himself neither subject nor accountable to anyone but God; [42] as he was above all earthly control, so he was bound only by the law of God and of nature.[43] The people, it is true, could at one time have been the actuating power, but they had ceded their rights. And Hayward referred to Bodin as showing that such a renunciation was actually extant in Rome, "graven in a stone." [44] The king was sovereign, then, but did he have any rights over the properties of his subjects? "It suffiseth to say with Seneca: 'the King has Empire, every man his particular property in all things.' " [45] Contracts between subject and king

---

[41] It should be said that Fullbeck had just caught Bodin in a contradiction on the question of the king's levying of imposts. The quotation is from Seneca. Fullbeck, *Pandects*, p. 70.

[42] Sir John Hayward, *An Answer to the First Part of a Certain Conference Concerning Succession etc.* (hereafter *An Answer*) (London, 1603), chap. v. For Hayward's life, see *D. N. B.*

[43] Hayward, *An Answer*, chap. v.

[44] *Ibid.*, chap. i.

[45] *Ibid.*, chap. iv.

had to be kept, and in the subject's case even if the king broke them.[46]

Here, then, was a pretty complete paraphrase of Bodin's thought. It is interesting to note that Bodin was used in such a fashion in England, to refute Parsons' allegation that there was a contract between the king and the people. It was, however, not only to refute Parsons himself that Hayward used Bodin's concept of sovereignty. He also used it to prove the king's superiority over religion in the state.

For how should he be esteemed a sovereign who in the greatest actions and affairs of State acknowledgeth the jurisdiction of another greater than himself . . . to correct his law, to restrain or control him.[47]

He then actually quoted Bodin to show the importance of undivided sovereignty.[48] Though property belonged to private persons, religion was undoubtedly the prerogative of sovereign monarchs.

Hayward thus adapted Bodin completely, although Fullbeck could not in the name of the common law, and Forsett was not able to do so in the name of an enhanced concept of sovereignty.

Forsett has with some exaggeration been called the "most original and distinguished of the political thinkers of the period from 1603 to 1642," apart from Thomas Hobbes.[49] He moved one step from Hayward and Bodin in his stress on the sovereign and in his omission of most of the *droit* element. God created the sovereign just as he created the soul in the human body.[50] Indeed, Forsett's whole argument is cast in the analogy of the human body (in itself not a very original scheme).[51] As the

[46] *Ibid.* Just as children are not free if the father breaks the contract. They cannot therefore dominate the father.

[47] Sir John Hayward, *A Report on a Discourse etc.* (hereafter *A Report*), (London, 1606), p. 11.

[48] *Ibid.*, p. 13.

[49] J. W. Allen, *English Political Thought, 1603–1660* (London: Methuen and Co., 1938), I, 83.

[50] Edward Forsett, *A Comparative Discourse etc.* (hereafter *Discourse*), (London, 1606), p. 6.

[51] This analogy was also used as an argument in favor of the union of England and Scotland. If the king is the head, let no one try to separate the two

soul rules the body by means of reason, so the sovereign rules the state by laws "which may no less aptly be termed the soul of sovereignty than reason is said to be the soul of the soul." [52] Obviously here Forsett put a great deal of emphasis upon the law and the sovereign power. These laws in enactment as well as in execution depended on the sovereign; the sovereign was the lawgiver.[53] Here the analogy to Bodin is obvious.

How was the sovereign then to be limited? Forsett swerved from the path of Jean Bodin: as an observer of English practice, as a member of Parliament, he knew that the king in England was not, properly speaking, the absolute lawgiver. Yet he did not therefore reject the idea of tangible sovereignty as his contemporary Fullbeck had done. Instead he limited the sovereign by the sovereign's own free will, not by independent law.

If the sovereign were uncorrupted, his will alone would undoubtedly be law unto itself. But the ruler was, after all, part of the human race, and as such might be misled by evil counsel. Therefore the sovereign should not take it upon himself alone to give the law, but should assemble his noblest and wisest subjects to advise with him in that action.[54] Moreover, just as best health was the health the body had from nature originally, so each kingdom was in better care when it held to its original constitution, laws, and customs.[55] This might limit the king, but inasmuch as there was no supernatural law to guarantee these limitations, but merely the ruler's good will, we have approached a doctrine of complete sovereignty. One has the feeling that with Forsett these limitations were but lip service to existing conditions. Bodin himself, looking at England, had found the whole sovereignty vested in Queen Elizabeth, one of

kingdoms. "For how can armes, legges and fette serve the head in the nourishment of the whole body, if they were only united in the head and divided amongst themselves?" Indeed man "is a little kingdom in himself." John Gordon, *A Sermon of the Union of Great Brittanie* (London, 1604), pp. 9, 10.

[52] Forsett, *Discourse*, p. 74.
[53] *Ibid.*, p. 74.
[54] *Ibid.*, pp. 16-17.
[55] *Ibid.*, p. 63.

the wisest and most virtuous princesses of the world.[56] Parliament was a mere advisory body and legal limitations upon the queen's prerogative were, to Bodin, nonexistent.[57]

The chief difference between Forsett and Smith or Morice earlier was the fact that Forsett's sovereign was not the King in Parliament, the High Court as final judge, but the king himself. True, he used the word "sovereign" rather than "king," but there was little doubt as to whom he meant. His discourse was printed by the king's printer, and James I rewarded him with the Manor of Tyburn for his services.[58]

It has been stated that Forsett derived his ideas not so much from Bodin as, "by some obscure process," from Plato, whom he quoted several times.[59] There was no need to go thus far afield. Quotations from the ancients were commonplace. Moreover, Forsett had, as we have seen, certain contacts with the Tudor tradition. He also surely had a great deal in common with Bodin: the sovereign as lawgiver, and the stress on the need of an ultimate authority somewhere in the state. Then, too, Forsett had something in common with Hooker in his stress on the "common good" as embodied in the sovereign. If we put Forsett beside Smith or Hooker, for example, he does not seem very original. In a manner, he too was at the crossroads.

Just as his contemporaries in France were stressing the power of the sovereign and minimizing his limitations, so Forsett in England was stressing the power of the ruler and minimizing his restraints. If he was more original than Smith, it was because Smith stressed the King in Parliament as a sovereign court, and Forsett obviously meant the king to be the lawgiver in the last resort. And, as lawgiver, the king was not limited by any superior power, but only by his own free will. This, of course, was to be a vital part of the idea of complete sovereignty, for

---

[56] Bodin, *La République etc.* (1593 edition), p. 1007. Elizabeth was "L'une des plus sages et virtueuse princesses du monde."

[57] *Ibid.*

[58] For a brief account of Forsett's life see *D. N. B.*

[59] Allen, *English Political Thought,* I, 83.

the ruler was not to be restrained by any superior being or abstract force.

We can realize when reading the words of a contemporary, the Bishop of Bristol, how far removed Forsett was from the medieval concept of a limited monarchy. Though a royalist preacher whose work advocating the union of England and Scotland had been read and approved by James, the bishop described his utopia in the following manner:

> The law enjoining obedience, and obedience executing the law, the prince cannot command what the people will **not obey, and** the people will obey what the prince **commandeth, and unity** among them will uphold all.[60]

But by 1604, even the good bishop held that the king might alter any law "on circumstances of time and occasion," though he was sworn by the coronation oath to keep the fundamental laws of the realm.[61] We have seen the attempt of three writers, at the turn of the century, to integrate into their thought the idea of sovereignty. Fullbeck clung to the idea of independent law and rejected the new concept. Like his contemporary, Sir Edward Coke, he could not fit the idea of sovereignty into the traditional framework of the constitution. Hayward paraphrased Bodin's formulation of sovereignty and retained the limitations which the Frenchman had put upon the sovereign. Forsett accepted the idea of sovereignty while rejecting the law as a binding limitation upon the sovereign: not the King in Parliament but the king limiting himself voluntarily.

It is to the development along the lines of Forsett's thought that we now turn. Once we have analyzed the idea of sovereignty as embodied in the royal person, we shall see that men like Whitelocke, in the tradition of the Tudor period, continued to vest increasing sovereignty in the King in Parliament. Finally, common lawyers, like Sir Edward Coke, rejected the idea of sovereignty, following the example of William Fullbeck.

[60] John Thornborough, *A Discourse Plainly Proving the Evident Utility etc.* (London, 1604), p. 32.
[61] *Ibid.*, pp. 17, 20.

III

THE KING AS SOVEREIGN

I

SIR WALTER RALEIGH provides the clearest instance of Bodinian influence on the English development of the idea of sovereignty as embodied in the royal person. Raleigh's principal political treatises were probably composed in the years 1603 to 1607. Of his acquaintance with Bodin there can be no doubt: the close agreement between Raleigh's thoughts and those of Jean Bodin has been shown by the convincing means of a textual comparison.[1] But it is typical of the difference between them that, where Bodin wrote, *"République est un droit gouvernement,"* Raleigh, in his paraphrase, omitted the word *droit*, and substituted the word "certain." A commonwealth, he wrote, is "a certain sovereign government of many families with those things that are common among them." [2] Thus we have here the germs of a most important development in theories of sovereignty. Bodin had been read, his ideas of sovereignty largely assimilated. But the element of *droit* so important in his writings seems to have dropped out.

---

[1] N. Kempner, *Raleghs Staatstheoretische Schriften* (Leipzig: Tauchnitz, 1928), pp. 68-74.
[2] *Ibid.*, p. 68.

Sovereignty, Raleigh maintained, is an absolute and perpetual power in every public state, and he is properly and only sovereign "that acknowledges no superior or equal, nor holdeth of any other prince, person or power but God and his own sword." [3] Raleigh's marks of sovereignty might have been copied from those of Bodin: the making or annulling of laws, the creation and disposition of magistrates, power over life and death, making of war and peace, highest or last appeal. [4] Raleigh then went on to apply these concepts to England, which he considered a royal monarchy like France. In a royal monarchy the subjects were obedient to the monarch's laws. [5] Here was drawn no contrast between England and France such as those which Fortescue and Smith had shown. In Raleigh's mind the two countries were of precisely the same sort. If such contemporaries of Raleigh as Sir Thomas Overbury and Robert Dallington realized that France was ruled by an absolute monarch, did that equating of England and France by Raleigh not presume that England too was an absolute monarchy? [6]

Such limitations as Raleigh placed on the king were purely voluntary (on the king's part) and utilitarian: natural law was totally absent. The monarch was to observe the laws of his country, not because they were a good in themselves, but because the people might otherwise be restless, especially if the king were to take away their commodities and bestow them on others. [7] Property was not really protected from the interference of the sovereign; instead the king was merely warned that if he touched it without cause, the people would grow intolerant of his rule.

In accounting for the existence of Parliament Raleigh again based his argument on its utility. The greatest security for the

[3] Sir Walter Raleigh, "The Cabinet Council," *Collected Works of Sir Walter Raleigh* (Oxford, 1829), VIII, 38. (Unless specifically indicated, all references to Raleigh's writings are taken from this edition and volume.)

[4] *Ibid.*, p. 38. See also "Maxims of State," p. 1.

[5] *Ibid.*, "Cabinet Council," p. 39.

[6] *Vide supra*, p. 31.

[7] Raleigh, "Maxims of State," p. 16.

prince was the willing obedience of the subject.[8] In all common-wealths, part of the government should be delegated to the people, lest they oppose the state, thinking themselves unimportant in it.[9] The king should, therefore, make it appear as if taxes were offered to him by the people, rather than exacted by him alone.[10] So far as parliamentary power itself was concerned, the king was its very soul, for a bill, to be legal, must have his assent, and his assent was valid only if given of his own free will, not if forced or influenced by pressure of one sort or another.[11]

The king as sovereign stood truly absolute. He was restrained only by the natural dictates of caution. He was the only lawgiver. This idea of sovereignty may be contrasted with the opinion voiced by Chief Justice Coke, with whom the king was not bound by any law either, save such law made in his realm "as by sufferance of your grace and your progenitors, the people of this your realm have taken at their free liberty by their own consent to be used amongst them." [12] Raleigh could not have considered a king so bound to be truly sovereign.

It is thus wrong to regard Raleigh as basically an advocate of mixed monarchy.[13] Parliament, the people's organ of participation in the making of law, was but a utilitarian device and not a binding precept upon the monarch. For Raleigh the only necessary part of the constitution seems to have been the king as lawgiver, using Parliament to be sure, but giving or withholding assent to the advisory body's recommendations at his own discretion, without obligation to accept them. We have seen that for Bodin himself the Parliament was a mere advisory body which did not limit the queen's prerogative.

Yet Raleigh seems not always consistent. How can the statement that wise men ought not to desire to live in a country

---

[8] *Ibid.*, p. 16.

[9] *Ibid.*, p. 3.

[10] *Ibid.*, p. 17.

[11] *Ibid.*, p. 170.

[12] Sir Edward Coke, *Second Institutes etc.* (London, 1797), Pt. I, p. 342.

[13] Zera Fink, *The Classical Republicans* (Evanston: Northwestern University Press, 1945), p. 23.

where men have more authority than the law be reconciled with his extreme view of sovereignty? [14] Moreover, in Raleigh's ideal state everyone might securely enjoy his own.[15] The explanation seems to be that, in common with most of his contemporaries, Raleigh was suspicious of new law. The sovereign should, if possible, maintain the old laws and temporize with such accidents as may make them invalid.[16] Raleigh, fearful of innovations of all kinds, believed that men should not be induced to believe new things until these innovations had been proved by experience.[17] The great Elizabethan shared his countrymen's suspicions of innovations in statecraft, of new laws rashly made to fit a temporary circumstance. The best commonwealth was an orderly and quiet state: "For God is the God of order and harmony and not confusion." [18] Raleigh opposed arbitrary government only because it resulted in confusion and civil strife. However, ". . . arbitrariness in a multitude is far more dangerous than in a single person." [19] Royal sovereignty, even in its absolutist sense, seemed to him more stable than any other form of government.

That law should have more authority than men should have need not mean that the sovereign should be under the law. He could still be the law's source and yet not change or alter laws and customs frequently, so that each might securely possess his own and confusion might be prevented. Maintaining the *status quo* might be the only politic thing to do in order that both ruler and people could live quietly and contentedly. Indeed, Raleigh stated that a prince showed his ruin to be near when he began to break ancient laws and customs that had long been obeyed by the people.[20]

[14] Raleigh, "Cabinet Council," p. 110.

[15] *Ibid.*

[16] *Ibid.*, p. 40.

[17] *Ibid.*, p. 100. Raleigh's regard for experience as the best teacher played into his great reverence for history as the vehicle for God's judgment, as he expressed it in the preface to his *History of the World*.

[18] Sir Walter Raleigh, *A Discourse of the Original and Fundamental Cause of Natural, Arbitrary, Necessary, and Unnatural War* (London, 1701), p. 99.

[19] *Ibid.*, p. 102.

[20] Raleigh, "Cabinet Council," p. 100.

Later, in the reign of Charles, Sir Peter Ball proposed the codification of the law of England on the grounds that public obedience and private security would be insured by such a measure. For, continued Henrietta Maria's solicitor general, nothing disquiets the people more at present than the fear and doubt of being deprived of their old laws.[21] Even King James expressed concern for the ancient and laudable customs of the realm. But for Ball and James, as for Raleigh, politic utility rather than the God-given principles of natural law determined their attitude towards the ancient laws and customs of England.

Here the element of utility seems once again to assert itself. It has been demonstrated that Raleigh's contention as to the desirability of maintaining old laws was a virtual paraphrase of a statement in the second chapter of Machiavelli's *Prince*.[22] Machiavelli's influence on Raleigh seems to have been at least as important as that of Bodin, and perhaps even more so. It goes without saying that Raleigh did not acknowledge his debt to Machiavelli. Rather, he openly condemned his doctrines.[23] But Raleigh surely had less justification for condemning Machiavelli than had Bodin, with his idea of *droit* government.[24] Raleigh's professions of regard for the old established laws can hardly be put alongside the legal theories of Fortescue or of Fullbeck.

It remains to be proved whether Machiavelli's emphasis on ancient laws and customs, if only for the sake of policy, did not exert some appreciable influence on those who championed those laws in England, whether the Italian did not, ironically,

[21] Sir Peter Ball, *Report on the Codification of the English Law* (British Museum, Malled 32096), pp. 177 ff.

[22] Kempner, *Raleghs Staatstheoretische Schriften*, p. 76.

[23] *Ibid.*, p. 25.

[24] This in spite of the fact that Dr. Kempner constantly equates Machiavelli and Bodin; she says nothing about the natural law elements in Bodin. *Ibid.*, p. 31. In a manner of speaking the element of utility underlies, of course, the whole development of the laws and customs themselves, thus "utilite ut necessitate" was one of the basic elements in the consulting of medieval estates in the matter of taxes and was only systematized into a political maxim by Machiavelli. Mario Praz also detects Botero's influence on Raleigh. Mario Praz, *Machiavelli in Inghilterra* (Rome: Tuminelli, 1943), p. 157. Botero is discussed on pages 52, 53.

underwrite part of the Tudor tradition. Certainly when Albertus Warren, in the Civil War, while all constitutional government was in hazard, appealed to the soldiers to uphold the common law in the name of self-interest lest their royalist holdings be endangered, he was championing the ancient law for reasons of policy.[25]

However, Raleigh's statement at his trial for treason in 1603 is difficult to integrate with his general ideas on government. "The wisdom of the law of God is absolute and perfect. . . but now by the wisdom of the State the wisdom of law is uncertain." [26] And yet to Raleigh the wisdom of the state as typified by the ruler was the highest sovereign power in the state. In 1603 Raleigh was fighting for his life. Surely this statement is relatively unimportant if measured against his more considered ideas of sovereignty. Perhaps, too, it might be conjectured, we have here merely a criticism of the manner in which the state was using the law—to spread uncertainty and confusion rather than to preserve that harmony and order which the ruler, if only for reasons of policy, should always further in the commonwealth.

It should be remembered that after his condemnation, Sir Walter Raleigh's mind seems to have turned increasingly toward God. The contemplation of the fall of mighty men (including his own) led Raleigh to enunciate the concept of God's overriding power and justice which we find in the preface to the *History of the World*. To Viscount Cranborn he wrote of his realization that "the best of men are but the spoils of time, and certain images wherewith childish fortune useth to play, kiss them today and break them tomorrow. . . ." [27] At the same time, he told the Earl of Salisbury that law ought not to override piety, but piety the law.[28] All this is in tune with his

[25] Albertus Warren, *Eight Reasons Categorical etc.* (London, 1653), p. 5. Similarly Sir Phillip Sidney followed Machiavelli's maxims in his warnings against changes in government. Irving Ribner, "Machiavelli and Sidney's *Discourse to the Queens Majesty*," *Italica*, XXVI (1949), 179, 186.

[26] *State Trials etc.*, ed. T. Howell (London, 1809), II, 18-20.

[27] British Museum, add. MSS. 6177, p. 153.

[28] *Ibid.*, p. 175.

assertion that the law of God is perfect and that the state has made the wisdom of the law uncertain. The Machiavellian Raleigh of the Irish campaigns was imprisoned in the tower; it is not surprising that his sentiments should have turned to the overriding power of God.[29] Yet he never denied the actual power of the sovereign of whom the laws of England are no less jealous than "Caesar was of Pompeia his wife." The king was still "superior" to the law.[30]

Sir Walter Raleigh's adaptation of the idea of sovereignty to the royal monarchy of England went even beyond Forsett's in its cogency. If it is true that his views were more representative than any lawyer's, that there were more people who thought as he did than not, then James's pretensions cannot have been so shocking to his contemporaries as they appear to have been to later historians.[31] Raleigh's biographers have found it difficult to reconcile the facts that the brave Tudor "sea dog" had fought so valiantly against Philip of Spain at the same time that he held such abhorrent absolutist ideas of government.[32] Excuses become futile and unnecessary once we realize that ideas of absolute royal sovereignty were not merely the quirks of a "foreign" king but were shared by many Englishmen as the idea of sovereignty came to be assimilated and accepted in English political thought. The only element necessary to make Raleigh's a "divine right of kings" theory was the divinity. This was, however, an important step in the development of the king's claim to sovereignty.

The divinity was added to the idea of sovereignty by royalist preachers like Roger Maynwaring. Laws to him too took their

---

[29] Praz, *Machiavelli in Inghilterra*, p. 161.

[30] British museum, add. MSS. 6177, p. 176. Letter to James I, rejecting the accusation of disloyalty.

[31] J. W. Allen, *English Political Thought, 1603–1660* (London: Methuen and Co., 1938), I, 67.

[32] Milton Waldman, *Sir Walter Raleigh* (New York: Harper and Brothers, 1928), p. 186. Parliamentary leaders liked the way in which Raleigh seemed to oppose both James and Spain. John Buchanan, *Sir Walter Raleigh* (Oxford: Clarendon Press, 1897), pp. 75 ff. Sir Robert Filmer, on the other hand, quotes Raleigh with approval on the iniquity of Magna Charta: Robert Filmer, *Free Holders Grand Inquest etc.* (London, 1647), I, 17.

force from the supreme will of the liege lord.[33] But he believed
that there existed also a higher body of law, the law of God.
This law was above the sovereign in all things. It was Bodin's
or Fortescue's law of God and nature reversed, for the prime
function of Maynwaring's law of God seemed to be to guarantee the ruler's sovereignty, not to limit it.[34] Indeed, his power
nowhere derived from the people, but was a direct emanation
from God himself. Neither the law of nations nor the territorial
law could limit the ruler's powers.[35] Human laws might not
detract from God's law, and God's law made the ruler sovereign
without let or hindrance.[36] Another divine, William Loe, who
had just returned from Hamburg, where differences with Laud
had driven him, extolled the sovereign power "vindicated from
all controllment." [37] He not only cited St. Peter, but preaching
before James, quoted Calvin to the effect that the king's decrees
have warrant from the mouth of Christ himself.[38]

For Maynwaring assemblies such as the Parliaments were
only useful for more equal exaction of taxes and of those duties
which belong by right to the king anyway.[39] And in a national
emergency, "reason of state" did not allow such assemblies to
meet.[40] Raleigh too had based some of the ruler's powers on the
idea of reason of state. For him, "The immortal policy of state
cannot admit any law or privilege, but in some peculiar it will
always be broken." [41] It becomes necessary, therefore, to consider the idea of reason of state, which, aiding the assimilation

[33] Roger Maynwaring, *Religion and Allegiance in Two Sermons* (London, 1627), Second Sermon, pp. 8-9.

[34] *Ibid.* See also, First Sermon, p. 23.

[35] *Ibid.,* Second Sermon, p. 13.

[36] *Ibid.,* p. 47. One of the favorite passages of preachers was the scriptural admonition: "Fear God, my sonne, and the King." Charles listened to this text twice within two months in 1627. Dr. Matthew Wren, *A Sermon etc.* (London, 1627), I 33. Isaac Bargrave, *A Sermon etc.* (London, 1627) pp. 2, 20.

[37] William Loe, *The Kings Shoe etc.* (London, 1623), p. 23.

[38] *Ibid.,* pp. 22, 27.

[39] Maynwaring, *Religion and Allegiance,* First Sermon, p. 26.

[40] *Ibid.,* First Sermon, p. 29.

[41] Raleigh, "The Prerogatives of Parliament," *Works,* VII, 198.

of the concept of sovereignty, played an important part in royalist as well as parliamentary thought.

2

The term "reason of state" first appeared in Italy in the sixteenth century.[42] It was a natural by-product of the conception of the state as a "work of art." Its rise as a concept is naturally associated with Machiavelli, who endowed the state with a moral personality of its own.[43] Bodin, as we saw, stressed the ruler's emergency powers in time of war, for then even property could be taken from the subject for reason of state as determined by the ruler. He gave, moreover, the idea a moral and legal basis by making reason of state, within due bounds, a content of the law of nature.[44] In contrast Fortescue also spoke of the "good publique." But he had not yet rationalized this into the idea of reason of state. "Good publique" meant the good of England, which was a *dominium politicum et regale.*[45] Emergency powers he allowed, but for emergencies only.

The vital germ of the idea of reason of state was surely the emergency power which the ruler exercised as protector of his people for the good of the community. Fortescue allowed such powers, as we have seen. Sir Julius Caesar was thus at least partly correct when, in 1610, he cited Fortescue as his authority for the fundamental law that in times of emergencies the people owed both service and goods to the king.[46] But to Caesar's master the idea of emergency power gave more ample scope in

[42] For an excellent discussion see Friedrich Meinecke, *Geschichte der Staatsraison in der neueren Geschichte* (Muenchen: R. Oldenbourg, 1929); also F. Wormuth, *Royal Prerogative 1603-1649* (Ithaca: Cornell University Press, 1939), pp. 73-77.

[43] Constantine D. Kojouharoff, "Niccolo Machiavelli; his contribution to the Social Sciences," *National University Law Review* (1930), pp. 21-81.

[44] Meinecke, *Geschichte der Staatsraison*, p. 73.

[45] Wilhelm Kleinecke, *Englische Fuerstenspiegel etc.* (Halle: Niemeyer, 1937), p. 169.

[46] Sir Julius Caesar, "On Ways and Means," in *Parliamentary Debates, 1610,* ed. S. R. Gardiner (Camden Society, 1879), p. 173.

governing than Fortescue had envisaged. Dr. Schramm has shown by his examination of coronation oaths that between the age of Fortescue and that of Caesar an important change occurred. Henry VIII regarded as his chief duty no more the preservation of peace alone, but the preservation of unity in church and people as well.[47] As preserver of the unity of the realm the king could easily claim an extension of emergency powers the extent of which even Smith later denied to the monarch by limiting his authority in times of rebellion.[48]

Reason of state was thus a weapon ready to hand for the monarch who wanted to capture sovereignty beyond the traditional limits defined by the constitution. The famous statement of Baron Fleming in the case of Bates that the "king's power is double, ordinary and absolute," and that the absolute power was that which "is applied to the general benefit of the people," [49] shows some of the danger which lay behind this concept. This absolute power, "most properly named policy and government," varied according to "the wisdom of the King for the common good." [50] Here, then, the king could extend his sphere of government into a direct invasion of the people's rights. Who was to say when an emergency existed? Could that idea not be expanded indefinitely when a responsible official like Bacon could write, "Necessity privileges only *quam jura privata* . . . against the Commonwealth necessity excuseth not: for *privilegium non valet contra republicam*." [51] To what extent this idea was ultimately expanded is well illustrated by a royalist pamphleteer writing in 1626. Since the king was the protector of the people, "Oh! Let not the people stand so much

[47] Percy Schramm, *A History of the English Coronation* (Oxford: The Clarendon Press, 1937), p. 216.

[48] *Vide supra*, chap. i.

[49] Baron Fleming in Bates's Case, *State Trials*, II, 389.

[50] *Ibid.*

[51] Sir Francis Bacon, "Maxims of Law," *Works of Sir Francis Bacon*, ed. Spedding and Heath (London, 1892), VII, 345. For an early instance of this maxim see the Abbot of Walton's case in *Tudor Studies*, ed. R. W. Seton-Watson (London: Longmans, Green and Co., 1924), pp. 176 ff. T. F. Plucknett holds that it did not have much effect at the time (p. 177).

upon the pretence of liberty, as to lose safety." It was, moreover, according to the law of nature that we should give tribute
to those who ministered to our common good.[52]

This was far removed from Fortescue's idea of the "good
publique." An Italian tract of the same year, translated by
William Vaughn and dedicated to the king, stated bluntly that
the author ". . . preferred the public peace of his government
before that strictness of justice which is mentioned in books." [53]
Ten years previously Englishmen could read, in translation, a
work by the Jesuit, Giovanni Botero, whom Meinecke credits
with making the idea of reason of state palatable to the princes
of the counterreformation by sweetening the harsh maxims of
Machiavelli.[54] Botero deplores violence and, calling necessity
violent, postulates that states cannot be maintained in such a
fashion. Godly council prevails above man's wit and policy.[55]
Wisdom is essential and this is part of true religion.[56] Botero
does not imply a rejection of the idea of reason of state, but he
does imply that such reason should be executed by those who
receive their wisdom from God through the Church. Thus,
and not by force, are nations maintained. Though his thought
served as an excellent guide to Catholic father-confessors of
European monarchs,[57] in England men like King James or

[52] Robert Sybthrope, *Apostolic Obedience etc.* (London, 1626), preface
and p. 4.

[53] Trajano Boccalini, *The New Found Politike, Disclosing the Secret Na-
tures and Dispositions etc.*, tr. William Vaughn (London, 1629), p. 167.

[54] Friedrich Meinecke, *Die Idee der Staatsraison* (Muenchen: R. Oldenbourg, 1925), p. 84.

[55] Giovanni Botero, *A Treatise Concerning the Causes of the Magnificencie
and Greatness of Cities*, tr. R. Petersen (London, 1606), pp. 36, 37, 38.

[56] *Ibid.*, p. 38.

[57] Friedrich Meinecke, *Die Idee der Staatsraison*, p. 86. Botero was concerned only "with the power and authority of the rulers and not with interests
of the subjects": Leonardo Olschki, *The Genius of Italy* (New York: Oxford
University Press, 1948), p. 432. For a discussion of Botero, see Luigi de Luca,
Stato e Chiesa nel Pensiero di G. Botero (Roma: Danesi Editore, 1946). In another translated work, Botero asked what could be more honorable in a
citizen, careful for the good of the state, than to extinguish dissension,
although he could not approve of Caesar because his wiles were too cunning,
and, one might add, not supervised by the Church. *Observations upon the
Lives of Alexander, Caesar, Scipio* (London, 1602). Italian concepts of the

Maynwaring believed in reason of state not because it was a doctrine of force, but because it implied the wisdom of the ruler obtained through communion with God. They heeded the admonition proclaimed by an advocate of James's succession to the English throne that without God's protection, no "policy will serve to keep you in seat." [58] Such a theory comes close to the views of Botero without the intrusion of the Catholic Church, which to the Italian was the true Church and therefore the guide to reason of state obtained through wisdom.

It was thus really only a step from the idea of the king as preserver of the unity of the Church and the people to James's rebuke to the House of Commons, "These are unfit things to be handled in Parliament, except your King should require it of you." It was of little use for members of Parliament to explain that if the king, of necessity, extended his prerogative, that was not sufficient ground to make it a right [59]—to which assertion Charles I, more cautious than his father, was to reply in 1629 (in answer to Parliament's accusation that he was levying tonnage and poundage illegally): "My intention was not to challenge tonnage and poundage as of right but *de bene esse:* showing you the necessity, not the right. . . ." [60]

By 1621, Parliament itself had been forced to adopt the idea of reason of state in order to counter the king. One member of Parliament remarked in 1610 that "law of State he knoweth not"; by 1621 the Commons asserted: "To reason of state and the preservation of state is most fit in this place." [61] Once it

idea of reason of state also infiltrated England through several works translated from the French, the most notable of which was Pierre Charron's *Of Wisdom* (London, 1612), which contained Bodin's formulation of sovereignty as well as an apology for the idea of reason of state, leaning heavily on Machiavelli.

[58] James P. R. Lyell, "A Tract on James VI's Succession to the English Throne," *English Historical Review*, LVI (1936), 292.

[59] *Parliamentary Debates*, 1610, ed. S. R. Gardiner (Camden Society, 1862), pp. 24, 83.

[60] *Commons Debates*, 1629, ed. Notestein and Relf (Minneapolis: University of Minnesota Press, 1921), p. 11.

[61] *Commons Debates*, 1621, ed. Notestein, Relf, Simpson (New Haven: Yale University Press, 1935), II, 492-493; Hedley in *Parliamentary Debates*, 1610, ed. S. R. Gardiner, p. 72. See also Tate, *ibid.*, pp. 83-84.

had taken over the concept, Parliament in turn began to elaborate and use it. In 1648, for example, the accusation against its nonrepresentative character was countered by the assertion that *salus populi,* not *vox populi,* was the supreme law, and that the people's welfare was in the custody of the King in Parliament.[62]

The assimilation of the idea of reason of state seems to have been a direct by-product of the struggle for sovereignty, symptomatic of the change in the constitution. Both the king in extending the idea and Parliament in taking it over left the old tradition behind.

Maynwaring may stand as typical of the royalist use of reason of state. As in Bodin, the idea was hallowed by God's law, but God's law to Maynwaring had the prime purpose of exalting the monarch and denuding the people of any rights whatsoever. It was with evident reluctance that Charles I, under parliamentary pressure, suppressed Maynwaring's sermons. While the preacher's work had drawn upon itself the understandable censure of the High Court of Parliament, yet, stated Charles, ". . . the grounds thereof were rightly laid, to persuade obedience from the subjects to their Sovereign, and that for conscience sake. . . ." [63] Another contemporary writer succeeded in combining the divinity of kings and reason of state in the spirit of Maynwaring. Arguing for the union of Scotland and England, he stated that the king was appointed by God to the "public weal of the whole island." He would therefore choose his servants on their merits alone, whether they came from one side of the Tweed or the other. How ridiculous to fear, therefore, that the king would prefer the Scots! Anyway, "All must be granted to a King: for that he is as God upon earth." [64]

---

[62] *Salus Populi solus Rex, The Peoples Safety is the Sole Sovereignty* (London, 1648), p. 18.

[63] *Royal Proclamation,* June, 1628, p. 20.

[64] Anon., *Rapta Tatio etc.* (London, 1604). Some writers, imbued with the idea of divine right of kings, even went as far as to condemn those "that study Bodin's *Commentaries,* Lipsius *Politics* . . . and such like quod libets, more than the holy scriptures." William Loe, *Vox Clamantis, a still Voice to the Three Estates of Parliament* (London, 1621), p. 61.

No longer was the idea of reason of state merely connected with the king's emergency powers as a necessary nuisance. Reason of state had come to mean more than just those limited emergency powers which the king possessed by virtue of his office. We have seen that with Raleigh, and even before, with Forsett, the prerogative was no longer a mere miscellaneous assortment of old feudal rights and pre-eminences which were limited by law. When a man like Staunford had written about the prerogative, he had defined it as the "privilege and pre-eminence that one person hath before another" only permitted in a "Prince or sovereign governor of the realm." Yet he went on to analyze this pre-eminence not in terms of the law of God but in terms of old feudal rights.[65] In Maynwaring, reason of state had received a moral basis as a part of God's law. And inasmuch as it had this basis, it was typical of the whole transformation of the idea of prerogative. The term "prerogative" had simply meant "pre-eminence" in the sense of certain customary rights enjoyed by one person and not by another. The royal prerogative was the pre-eminence which the king, by virtue of his office, enjoyed over his subjects. But the royal prerogative was far from absolute; instead it was a series of customary, feudal rights and nothing more than that.

By 1590 Staunford's analysis was already outdated, though typically enough Coke much later was to find high praise for Staunford's work.[66] Where men like Raleigh tried merely to find the highest power in the state without invoking a divine sanction, Maynwaring and the other royalists increasingly gave a moral basis to the king's claim to absolute sovereignty. Feudal rights were as nothing before the right of God witnessed by God's representative on earth. Thus the king's rights were "divine," as God-sanctioned as the natural law had been of old. The divine right of kings knew no earthly limitations. As for Chief Justice Coke, "Necessity is a brazen wall, *Lex tem-*

[65] Sir William Staunford, *An Exposition of the Kings Prerogative etc.* (London, 1590), see especially chap. 1.

[66] Not until the great debate on the Petition of Right did Coke abandon his unquestioning faith in Staunford. Frances H. Relf, *The Petition of Right* (Minneapolis: University of Minnesota Press, 1917), p. 14.

poris." [67] But for the king as well as for the writers we have analyzed, it was not a brazen wall but a vital requisite to the all-embracing sovereignty of the king. With Maynwaring, moreover, the ruler was not only completely sovereign but was actually an emanation from God himself. We have here one of the ultimate expressions of complete sovereignty. True, the ruler must not transgress God's law, as Nebuchadnezzar did, but that surely was a feeble limitation, for God's law enjoined first of all the absolutism of kings.[68]

With Maynwaring and with Raleigh we have traveled a considerable distance from Jean Bodin. With them the king, not the King in Parliament, has engulfed all sovereignty to the elimination of all *droit*. We seem to be approaching a position which William Shakespeare, good Elizabethan that he was, had envisaged with apprehension in his *Troilus and Cressida*, acted before London audiences in 1609:

> Force should be right; or rather, right and wrong
> (Between whose endless jar justice resides)
> Should lose their names, and so should justice too.
> Then everything includes itself in power,
> Power into will, will into appetite.[69]

[67] *Parliamentary Debates*, 1625, ed. S. R. Gardiner (Camden Society, 1879), p. 85.

[68] Maynwaring, *Religion and Allegiance in Two Sermons*, First Sermon, p. 149.

[69] William Shakespeare, *Troilus and Cressida*, I, 3 (117-120). For a discussion of Ulysses' speech in its Tudor background, see J. E. Phillips, *The State in Shakespeare's Greek and Roman Plays* (New York: Columbia University Press, 1940), pp. 77 ff., 120 ff.

IV

ENGLAND'S GOD ON EARTH [1]

I

How did the ideas of James I fit with the concepts of royal sovereignty which were being elaborated all around him? Was his a really thoroughgoing application of the idea of royal sovereignty as presented by Raleigh and Maynwaring? In order to grasp the real measure of James's pretensions it will be necessary to ascertain his views concerning those "chief marks of sovereign power" which, as we have seen, were held in common by Bodin and Raleigh.

James's ideas have too often been treated in isolation. It must never be overlooked that James came from Scotland, and that when he ascended the English throne he was a man in the middle span of life, with his ideas already largely set. During his rule in Scotland one of his main problems had been the re-establishment of the royal authority, which he had accomplished by successfully playing faction against faction.[2] But his experience in Scotland proved a handicap to him when he had to deal

---

[1] Robert Pricket, *A Souldiers Resolution* (London, 1603), p. 10.

[2] For the account of James's Scottish experiences, see Helen G. Stafford, *James VI of Scotland and the Throne of England* (New York: D. Appleton-Century, 1940), p. 292.

with English affairs, for he was too eager to equate the institutions of the two countries.

This inclination appeared in his *True Law of Free Monarchies*, written five years before he ascended the throne of England. In Scotland, James wrote, laws were not established before the appearance of a king on the national scene. The kings of Scotland came over from Ireland originally, and made and established the laws as well as the estate and form of the government. Therefore kings were the authors and makers of laws, and not the laws the makers of the king. The king was the overlord of the realm without advice of Parliament or "any subaltern judicial seat." The same, in James's opinion, held true of England and of all other free monarchies.[3] Had not the Bastard of Normandy come over to England with a huge army, there to take the island by force—"Where he gave the law and took none, changed the laws [and] inverted the order of Government?"[4] There is little doubt, then, that before he came to England James VI of Scotland considered himself the lawgiver of his country, and expected to apply the same principles to the land that would soon be his new kingdom. The question whether he adjusted his theories to his new kingdom, when he became James I of England, merits consideration. Did he change his opinions after he became James I of England?

In 1607 we find James once more dwelling on the origin of the state by royal conquest.

> Yet how soon kingdoms began to be settled in civility and polity, then did kings set down their minds by laws, which are properly made by the king only; but at the rogation of the people, the king's grant being obtained thereunto.[5]

Here the king was still properly the maker of the law, but at the rogation of his people: surely these are the germs of an ad-

---

[3] James I, "True Law of Free Monarchies," *The Political Works of James I*, ed. C. H. McIlwain (Cambridge, Mass.: Harvard University Press, 1918), p. 62. (All subsequent citations from James's works are taken from this edition, unless otherwise indicated.)

[4] *Ibid.*, p. 63.

[5] James I, "Speech of 1607," p. 309.

justment to the English Parliament. After ruling for three years, James felt that he could evaluate the place of Parliament in the constitution; "this highest court of Parliament it is nothing else but the King's great council, which the King does assemble either upon occasion of interpreting, or abrogating old laws, or of making new. . . ." [6] By 1621, nineteen years after the last statement, James did not seem to have changed his opinions. Parliaments were instituted long after monarchies were created. When people began to be willing to be guided by laws, then came the first institution of Parliament. Parliament existed in order to give the king advice in such errands as he should command.[7] It was thus called to give advice and assistance to the king in the ". . . continuance and further settling of the peaceable government and safety of this kingdom, whereof God has given us charge. . . ." [8]

It is clear that James regarded himself as the lawgiver, and Parliament merely as an advisory body. But it is equally evident that James, overtly, never claimed the power to make or change laws without the advice of Parliament. At least, in 1621 as in 1603, he reiterated that making laws could only properly proceed in Parliament.[9] In spite of the fact that Parliament was here reduced to an advisory body with no independent powers apart from the king's own moving power, James seems to have made at least some concessions to English conditions, if only to persuade Parliament to supply his wants with more alacrity. Was the king then in theory bound by any superior body of law to make laws *only* in Parliament? James's opinion of the necessity of Parliament's "concurrent consent," taken by itself, might have had Fortescue's entire approval.

There was for James, too, a law that was above all human law—the law of God.[10] Human laws must conform to that law:

[6] James I, "Speech of 1605," pp. 287-288.

[7] *Commons Debates,* 1621, ed. Notestein, Relf, Simpson (New Haven: Yale University Press, 1935), II, 4.

[8] *Royal Proclamation,* 6 November, 1620.

[9] James I, "Speech of 1603," p. 277; *Commons Debates,* 1621, ed. Notestein, Relf, Simpson, II, 6.

[10] James I, "Speech of 1616," p. 330.

otherwise they were unjust and illegal. God's law "hath given me the honour to prescribe laws at home for my subjects." [11] There is nothing here about the advisory capacity of Parliament or the sanctity of personal rights. Indeed, the content of God's law was justified in Bodinian terms: "In temporal matters, how can one person be sovereign, that may be fleeced of his temporalities by any superior power?" [12] As James asserted before Parliament itself, shortly after his accession to the throne, the calling of Parliament sprang purely out of the king's grace. [13] How could such representation be the "birthright of the subject" when the law of God, which was above all human restraint, gave to the king the power to prescribe laws for his subjects? [14]

Thus without much doubt James considered himself the only lawgiver. He agreed with that Englishman who, utterly divorced from all bonds of precedent in his native country, greeted his new sovereign with the statement that,

> The Laws of England will themselves derive
> From great King James his high Prerogative. [15]

It was merely a peculiar custom of the land that prompted the calling of Parliament. And as James confided to the Spanish ambassador, he found the custom when he came to England and could not change it. [16] If with Scottish shrewdness he made the best of the necessary evil, so with Scottish stubbornness he never regarded Parliament as more than an advisory body. As late as 1621 he still lectured Parliament: "The King, he is the maker of [the laws] and you are the advisors, councilors, and confirmers of them." [17]

---

[11] James I, "The Rights of Kings," p. 169.

[12] *Ibid.*, p. 170.

[13] James I, "Speech of 1605," p. 287.

[14] James I, "The Rights of Kings," p. 169.

[15] Robert Pricket, *A Souldiers wish unto his sovereign Lord King James* (n.p., 1603).

[16] S. R. Gardiner, *History of England, 1603–1642* (London: Longmans, Green and Co., 1883), II, 251.

[17] *Commons Debates, 1621*, ed. Notestein, Relf, Simpson, II, 4.

Thus far James followed the Bodinian pattern. Bodin, too, had conceded that the ruler might take the estates into his confidence.[18] But from here on, James, like Raleigh or Forsett, diverged from the concept of sovereignty expounded by the French lawyer. Contracts were sacred to Bodin under the law of nature. James, too, dwelled on the sacredness of contracts; he included in this category the coronation oath, ". . . the fundamental law by which the King's office is defined." [19] But, arguing from the concept of sovereignty, he asked who should judge if the king were to break it. Only God could be judge, naturally, because otherwise a subject or judge would be able to constitute a superior power over the king.[20] The king alone could decide how a contract with his subjects should be kept; he was the father of his people. By means of this dialectic the sanctity of contracts between sovereign and subject was whittled away.

In order to understand James's views on the sanctity of the subject's property, we must look more closely at his concept of the natural law. James, too, believed in a law of nature. "By the law of nature," wrote James, "the King becomes a natural father to his lieges," [21] and the king's power under the law of nature derives from that of the father.[22] To Bodin, too, the *patria potestas* was the origin of all superior power. But James drew from this a totally different conclusion from that of Bodin. The transformation of the family into the state had not changed the basic concept of the *patria potestas*. As the father could dispose of the inheritance of his children at his pleasure, so might the king deal with his subjects.[23] Men, James held, by the law of nature owe their allegiance first to their countries, then to their families, and lastly to themselves.[24]

Royalist writers followed James in drawing similar conclu-

---

[18] *Vide supra*, p. 39.
[19] James I, "True Law of Free Monarchies," p. 55.
[20] *Ibid.*, p. 65.
[21] *Ibid.*, p. 55.
[22] James I, "Speech of 1607," p. 308.
[23] *Ibid.*, p. 308.
[24] *A Publication of His Majesties Edict etc.* (London, 1613), p. 113.

sions based on the analogy of the father to the king. One writer
asserted that there was indeed a higher bond between the children and the father of the country than between fathers and
children in merely private families. Here again the king's duty
of protection was stressed. The obedience of the subject was
grounded on the law of nature, "for as we be born sons, so are
we born subjects." [25] James liked this treatise so well that he
issued a proclamation to spread the teaching and publishing of
this "perspicious" book.[26]

Thus natural law was twisted beyond all recognition. Instead of protecting the subject, it bolstered the arbitrary claims
of the monarch. Here we have a concept in tune with the development which we have seen in Forsett, Raleigh, and Maynwaring.[27] Perhaps it could even be said that here was harvested
the weakening of the medieval natural law which we saw beginning in the Tudor days.

Contrast James's conclusion as to the inheritance of his subjects with Coke's dictum that "The common law hath so admeasured the prerogative of the king, as he cannot take nor
prejudice the inheritance of any: and the best inheritance the
subject hath, is the law of the realm." [28] One might well ask
whether for James the sinews of the commonwealth, the law
of England itself, had any meaning. It seems as if he regarded
the common law as he regarded Parliament, as an inevitable
nuisance which the king had to make the best of. Here his
Scottish background becomes once more significant.

James admired the civil law of his native land. That admira-
tion by itself is nothing very surprising, for Englishmen themselves generally had a high regard for the law of Rome, which
they seem to have regarded as the equivalent of the English

---

[25] Robert Mockett, *God and the King* (London, 1615), p. 81.

[26] *Royal Proclamation*, 13 November, 1615.

[27] It was only some forty years earlier that Burleigh had proudly written
on behalf of Queen Elizabeth's government, ". . . we have never sought life,
blood, the goods, the houses, states or lands of any person in any estate or
degree." "A Declaration of the Queen's Proceedings since her Reign," *A Col-
lection of State Papers Left by William Cecil* (London, 1740–59), I, 590.

[28] Sir Edward Coke, *Second Institutes etc.* (London, 1797), I, 62.

common law. "The common law, to speak precisely, is our civil law," wrote Gabriel Harvey to Sir Thomas Smith.[29] Smith himself, as we saw above, held a similar view of the civil law. He had been trained in the civil law at Padua and was to become professor of civil law at Cambridge. Yet in his inaugural lecture at Cambridge the technicalities of the civil law were derided and the eloquence and vigor of the common law courts were praised.[30] After all, it was the common law, the civil law of England, which guaranteed the liberty of Englishmen.

Civil law and common law thus do not seem to have been antagonistic to each other in the views of Smith or, for that matter, of Fortescue. Hooker, too, had words of praise for the civil law.[31] Fullbeck in turn, as we have seen, a devoted common lawyer, recommended the reading of the civil law.[32] Indeed, he, like Sir John Doderidge and many other lawyers, compared the two bodies of law in order to find some common ground between them. When the struggle between king and Parliament was joined, we at times find even parliamentarians appealing to the civil law (when it suited their purposes). James must have been surprised when the opposition in the case of the Post Nati based its argument partly on Roman law: "Quando duo jura concurrent in una persona aequum est acsi essent in diversis." [33] In 1621, in Floyd's case, the House based its position, in extending its jurisdiction, on the idea that "an offense against the king *quoniam ipse* [saith the Emperor] *pars corporis nostri sunt* etc." [34] As late as 1621 Sir Edwin Sandys praised the civil law as the best resort in testamentary matters.[35]

To James, however, the civil law seems to have been more than just the equivalent of the common law in foreign coun-

[29] *Letterbook of Gabriel Harvey*, ed. E. G. L. Scott (Camden Society, 1884), p. 164.

[30] Wm. Mullinger, *The University of Cambridge etc.* (Cambridge: Cambridge University Press, 1884), II, 132, 219.

[31] *Vide supra*, p. 23, fn. 53.

[32] William Fullbeck, *The Panedects of the Law of Nations* (London, 1603), pp. 68, 69.

[33] *State Trials etc.*, ed. T. Howell (London, 1809), II, 687.

[34] *Commons Debates*, 1621, ed. Notestein, Relf, Simpson, II, 353.

[35] *Ibid.*, IV, 218.

tries. Directly after the law of God came the law of nations. In 1607, before James had, in his own words, any great acquaintance with the common law, he identified the civil law of Rome with the law of nations.[36] Where the law of the land was not clear, recourse was to be had to the civil law, James implied, and thereafter, when there was no positive law, to the king himself, for he was, in that case, *lex loquens*.[37] In accordance with his view on sovereignty, he delegated himself as the ultimate lawgiver. The civil law as the law of nations played a very important part in James's legal ideas. The identification of the law of nations with the Roman law was again not uncommon amongst Englishmen. We find on occasion even as stout a parliamentarian as Sir Edwin Sandys appealing to the law of nations and equating it with the civil law.

But for James, the law of nations itself was equivalent to the law of nature, as coming directly after the law of God.[38] Thus we have, in effect, the law of nature equated with the Roman law rather than with the common law of England. It should be added that James quickly ended his speech of 1607 referring to the Roman law by stating that he knew only what belonged to a king, and would press no further.[39] Politic modesty.

In 1616, James restated his belief in the civil law as, together with the common law, a part of the law of nations. But by now he was more politic and did not imply therein the sweeping powers of a superior law of last appeal. He put the common law on an equal footing with the civil law, both being beneath the law of God. Lord Chancellor Ellesmere found himself in agreement with this view.[40] Earlier, in 1609, James had already stated that the "Civil law is in a manner *ius gentium*," but that he

[36] James I, "Speech of 1607," p. 299.

[37] *Ibid*. Thomas Ridley, a divine, also suggested that civil law might be used for matters not covered by common law. *A View of the Civil and Ecclesiastical Law* (Oxford, 1634), p. 225. Sir Robert Wiseman put forward a similar argument during the Protectorate, *The Law Of Laws* (London, 1656).

[38] *A Publication of his Majesties Edict and Severe Censure against Private Combats and Combatants* (London, 1613), p. 3.

[39] James I, "Speech of 1607," p. 299.

[40] James I, "Speech of 1616," p. 331. For Ellesmere's opinion, see Case of Post Nati, *State Trials etc.*, II, 670, 672.

would restrain it within the bounds which the common law allowed.[41] It seems evident that James, on the whole, thought of the civil law as the law of nations, which in Scotland supplemented the law whenever the municipal law was defective.

Here, though, James was not without confusion, not above distinguishing one point between the civil law and the law of nations.[42] These vacillations before Parliament may have been in the interest of policy. He could not have been unaware of the growing antagonism to the civil law in favor of the rival jurisdiction of the common law courts, as well as of Parliament's growing hostility to his own person. The episode of Cowell's *Interpreter* shows James's position more clearly.

John Cowell, a civil lawyer, had attempted to force the common law into the pattern of Justinian's *Institutes*. The king to him was above the ordinary course of the common law. Yet his ideas were not so extreme when taken as a whole. It was true that all those regalities which belonged to the most absolute prince in the world also belonged to the English king. Yet, by the custom of the country, the king in England "maketh no law without the consent of the three estates, though he may squash any law concluded by them." [43] So far as the actual functions of Parliament were concerned, he referred the readers of his law dictionary, the *Interpreter*, to Sir Thomas Smith's *Republica*.[44]

Surely, here Parliament had no mean place in the working of the constitution. Indeed, Cowell went so far as to declare that the king by his coronation oath swore to keep the customs of England intact.[45] On the other hand, the customs of the country and the summoning of Parliament to make laws were no inherent birthright of the people, and their preservation sprang from the mercy of the king.[46] The king was always *legibus superior* in that he was able to confer privileges by his

[41] James I, "Speech of 1609," p. 310.
[42] James I, "Speech of 1607," pp. 300-302.
[43] John Cowell, "Prerogative of the King," *The Interpreter* (London, 1637).
[44] *Ibid.* "Parliament."
[45] John Cowell, *Institutiones etc.* (Cambridge, 1605), p. 6.
[46] Cowell, "Parliament," *The Interpreter.*

own volition. Moreover, he was also the interpreter of the law.[47] But the fact remains that "in peace the King does not make any laws but by consent of the three estates in Parliament." [48] Do we not have here, too, an adjustment to the existing customs of England?

With Cowell's attiude toward the Roman law, James must have been in agreement. Roman and common law sprang from the same foundations, we find in the *Interpreter*,[49] while in his *Institutiones* Cowell dwelled on the universal nature of the civil law. And like writers such as Thomas Ridley, he intimated that it might be used as a law of appeal in cases where the common law was weak.[50] In view of Cowell's doctrines, would it be too much to maintain that an angry Parliament used the civil lawyer as a whipping boy for some of his master's theories?

James's repudiation of the book was manifestly undertaken under Parliament's pressure, especially since there was a great similarity between the views of Cowell and those of the king. If James condemned the book as being too bold with the common law of the land, he also condemned it as wading further into the prerogative "than is fit for a subject." [51] Would it be too much to assume also that the latter condemnation was the genuine one? If we are to trust to report, James's real views of the two systems of law were more likely expressed at dinner, when he extolled the civil law well above the common law.[52]

It is clear that James had to adjust himself to the existence of the common law. In his proclamations he took many an occa-

---

[47] Cowell, *Institutiones etc.*, p. 5.

[48] Cowell, "Martial Law," *The Interpreter* (1607).

[49] *Ibid.* Preface to the Reader.

[50] Cowell, *Institutiones etc.*, p. 15, and *Praefatio*. For Thomas Ridley, see n. 88. Both Cowell and Ridley mention family law as the particular province where civil law could improve over the common law. See also S. B. Chrimes, "The Constitutional Ideas of Dr. John Cowell," *English Historical Review*, LXIV (October, 1949), 461-468.

[51] *Parliamentary Debates*, 1610, ed. S. R. Gardiner (Camden Society, 1879), p. 23.

[52] James I, *Political Works*, App. B, p. lxxxvii.

sion to affirm "how desirous we have always been to renew and revive the ancient and laudable customs of this our kingdom. . . ." [53] He could not attempt to introduce the civil law even as a law in "the last resort" identical with the law of nations.

To cope with the common law, therefore, James began to stress his own position as highest judge of that law: Bodin's last appeal as a mark of sovereignty. We have already seen an instance where he stressed the function of the king himself as *lex loquens* and as last court of appeal when all written law had failed. Indeed, kings were properly judges, for they sat in the throne of God from whence all judgments were derived. The greatest part of the king's office lay in deciding the *meum et tuum* of his subjects.[54] Revenging of private wrong belonged to the king, to whom God has committed the sword for precisely that purpose. Thus, private revenge, such as duelling, was a crime against the king's majesty itself, to be punished by the Star Chamber.[55] What relation did a king so exalted in judicature have to the law which was made, even in James's theory of sovereignty, with the advice of Parliament?

Here James stressed the idea of reason of state. Hooker would no doubt have been horrified to behold how the king, in the name of the common good, claimed to set aside laws which public opinion had made. Said James (even before he came to the English throne), although it is true that the king is above the law, as its author, yet he will conform himself and his actions to the law. But he must always remember that the health of the commonwealth is his chief concern—and where he sees the law doubtful and rigorous, he may interpret the same, lest otherwise *summum jus* be *summa iniuria*.

[53] *Royal Proclamation*, 8 April, 1617. See also, for example, *Royal Proclamation*, 6 November, 1620, where James makes a point of lawful freedom in election to Parliament according to the "laudable" laws and customs of the realm, p. 4.

[54] James I, "Basilikon Doron," p. 22.

[55] *Royal Proclamation*, 15 October, 1613.

And therefore general laws, made public in Parliament, may upon known respects to the king by his authority be mitigated, and suspended upon causes only known to him.[56]

As James restated it in 1613, it belonged to his royal clemency to moderate and mitigate the rigor of the laws.[57] It is significant that Chancellor Ellesmere crossed out from the speaker's personal address to James in 1614 this particular sentence:

Demand, O Sovereign, the strict operation of the laws and suffer no occasion, no restraint therein whatsoever, for the life and soul of law consists in the operation of the law. . . .[58]

Thus James made full use of the idea of reason of state which, as we have seen, lay ready to hand. Cutting through the tangle of law and Parliament, James affirmed that "the health of the commonwealth be his chief law." [59]

Truly the king had the last appeal in judicial matters. James may have spoken of the "High Court of Parliament," but to him that advisory body was not the last court of appeal. The king in James's eyes thus obviously had the chief marks of sovereignty, the making and annulling of laws—highest appeal.

The king also had the power to appoint all magistrates. The grant of an office in medieval England was the same as a grant of land. It conferred an estate in the office and its emoluments.[60] As recently as the reign of Queen Elizabeth we have the case of Cavendish, whom the judges, against the queen's express command, refused to deprive of his office in the court of law because he had an "estate in it." [61] Thus customary rights triumphed even over the commands of the great queen. However, Sir Thomas Smith had stated before the case of Cavendish that the king had the right to appoint the chief officers

[56] James I, "True Law of Free Monarchies," p. 63.

[57] *Royal Proclamation*, 20 March, 1614.

[58] Personal address to James I by the speaker of Parliament (1614), 4. El. 2608, (El. signifies Ellesmere MSS. at the Henry E. Huntington Library).

[59] James I, "True Law of Free Monarchies," p. 63.

[60] C. H. McIlwain, "The Tenure of English Judges," *Constitutionalism and the Changing World* (New York: Macmillan, 1939), p. 295.

[61] Cavendish's Case, *State Trials etc.*, pp. 11, 629 ff.

and magistrates: this was expressly within his particular sphere of power.[62] Moreover, ever since the earliest times the judges had held their patents *quamdiu nobis placuerit*, with the exception of the barons of the exchequer.[63] James thus at his accession could appoint most judges by his own free will.

But there was here a deeper problem involved: the judges were the interpreters and representatives of the common law. James was therefore naturally desirous of circumventing their power and of fitting their ideas into his concepts of prerogative and sovereignty. By stressing his position as supreme judge as well as lawgiver he was able to depreciate the position of the judges. "As kings borrow their power from God, so judges from kings." [64] In settled monarchies, where law was established formally and in an orderly fashion, the right of judgment was given by kings to subordinate magistrates—not that the king divested himself of his function, but that he delegated it to them temporarily and conditionally.[65] Indeed, the judges were his "councilors" in matter of judicature, just as Parliament was in the making of law. James thus put great stress on the oath of the judges requiring them to advise the monarch.[66]

James stated purposefully that, though laws were in many places obscure, yet the judges' interpretation must always be subject to common law and reason. "For I will never trust any interpretation that agreeth not with common sense or reason, and true logic, for *ratio est anima legis* in all human laws." [67] *Ratio est anima legis;* with this sentence Coke too concluded his *First Institute*, but Coke's ratio was that knowledge of reason which could only come from the study of the law, and which would always be inaccessible to James, who had not been trained at the Inns of Court.

[62] *Vide supra*, chap. i.
[63] McIlwain, *Constitutionalism in a Changing World*, pp. 297, 298.
[64] James I, "Speech of 1616," p. 327.
[65] *Ibid.*
[66] James I, Letters of the Judges, "Tracts relating to Commendams," in *Works of Sir Francis Bacon*, ed. Basil Montagu (London, 1827), p. 325.
[67] James I, "Speech of 1616," p. 332.

Insofar as Coke was concerned, this very fact, as we shall see, disqualified James as judge of any sort.[68] No wonder James complained, "As for reason, that is so large a thing [with common lawyers] as that a man knows not where to pitch." [69] To this Coke might have answered that he was not supposed to know.

In consequence of his opposition to legal reason, James began to take up a cause which was during the revolution to become a greater and more pressing issue. If the law were precise, written so that all could know it, the idea of legal reason and the pretensions of the judges would be devoid of meaning. They would then in all truth be just subordinate magistrates. Thus James wished that the law were written in the vulgar tongue,

". . . for now it is in an old, mixed and corrupt language only understood by lawyers, whereas every subject ought to understand the law under which he lives." [70]

Again, Parliament should select and approve all cases to be used as precedent for all time to come. Thus the great variety of cases and precedents, as well as much of the obscurity in the law, would be avoided. On the other hand, just before ascending the throne of England, James had asserted that the prince alone must take action in order that evil custom does not become known as good law.[71] "Yet better it is to have a certain law with some spots in it, nor live under such an uncertain and arbitrary law. . . ." [72] Is this not reminiscent of the later position of Sir Matthew Hale that certain law, though accompanied by some mischief, was preferable to arbitrary government? Only, to Hale the best quality of this "certain law" was its

---

[68] *Vide infra*, chap. viii.

[69] *Commons Debates*, 1621, ed. Notestein, Relf, Simpson, II, 343.

[70] James I, "Speech of 1609," p. 311.

[71] James I, *Deamonologiet etc.* (London, 1603), p. 25.

[72] James I, "Speech of 1607," pp. 292-293. In the same speech James made the statement, ". . . for you all know, *rex est lex loquens*. . . ," p. 291.

all-important function of protecting the subject against arbitrary might.[73]

James wanted a certain law to eliminate the independent claims of the judges and to subordinate them completely to his will. Thus while in Hale's time a certain law was a guarantee against despotic government, in James's time the quest for a certain law was the advancement of the king's pretensions to absolute sovereignty, for it eliminated the independence of the judges and it qualified the king to interpret all law—for he, too, had "common sense." James, then, claimed all the marks of sovereignty under his dual role of lawmaker and supreme judge: Parliament and the judges were merely advisory bodies.

Against the growing pretensions of Parliament, James began to elaborate a kind of "legal reason" of his own. The king's power of prerogative should not be touched by Parliament because this matter was a "mystery of state." [74] It was dangerous, he warned the Commons, to submit the king's power to any kind of definition.[75] It was not to be disputed what a king might do, but only "what a good king should do." He knew that the lower house was not a place to determine the law in case of private persons, "much less concerning a prince's right." [76] One cannot help feeling that from James's point of view these were thoroughly sensible statements, for a king, being truly the supreme power in the realm, and possessing all the "marks" of sovereignty, should not be subject to discussion by any inferior power.

Yet it must never be forgotten that James always recognized Parliament's claim to be consulted in the actual making of law. Indeed, in 1610 James admitted before Parliament that he had no power to exact subsidies without the consent of the three

---

[73] Sir Matthew Hale, "Reflections on Mr. Hobbes Dialogue of Law," in W. S. Holdsworth, *History of English Law* (Boston: Little, Brown & Co., 1927), IV, 509. George L. Mosse, "Thomas Hobbes: Jurisprudence at the Crossroads," *University of Toronto Quarterly*, XV (July, 1946), 350 ff.

[74] *Parliamentary Debates*, 1610, ed. S. R. Gardiner (Camden Society, 1879), p. 35. See also James I, "Speech of 1616," p. 333.

[75] *Parliamentary Debates*, 1610, ed. Gardiner (1879), p. 24.

[76] *Ibid.*, p. 153.

estates—and that *de jure*.[77] This statement is in manifest conflict with James's assertion, quoted above, that as father of his people he could dispose of inheritances.[78]

In this instance, as in his condemnation of Cowell's *Interpreter*, James was making concessions to the "local" sentiments of England. There seems to have been in James's character a mixture of Scottish stubbornness and of the canniness to make concessions if the need be. But these concessions, which James felt to be necessary adjustments to English conditions, never affected the basis of his political thought. There was to him no contradiction implied between his belief that on the one hand he could dispose of his subjects' properties and yet at the same time consult and obtain the consent of Parliament for all subsidies and that *de jure*, for *de jure* did not mean for James what it had meant for Jean Bodin: it was not a concept of *droit gouvernement* protected by the law of nature. *De jure* for James meant by his own law, springing from his power as sovereign and in the making of which Parliament had been consulted as "of grace." The good king, who is not a tyrant, ruled by his own laws.[79] And James was sure that he was no tyrant; and so he could harmonize Parliament's power of the purse as well as its participation in the making of law with his own theory of complete sovereignty.

In the mind of James, as in the minds of Raleigh and of Maynwaring, the sovereign was enhanced and the *droit* was virtually eliminated in government. The law of God decreed the superiority of kings, and the law of nature set the measure by making the father the complete lord over his family.

James as an active statesman had, as we saw, to rationalize the existence of the English Parliament and of the common law into his theory of sovereignty. There is here the same element of utility in accounting for these institutions as we found in Raleigh. It is somewhat ironic that the martyr of the "Spanish

[77] *Ibid.*, p. 24.
[78] *Vide supra*, p. 61.
[79] James I, "Speech of 1609," p. 309.

tyranny" and his persecutor should have a common theory of government. Indeed, James's apology for Raleigh's death, written by Bacon, began with the words, "Kings are not bound to give account of their actions to any but God alone," [80] a sentiment with which Raleigh would have been in full agreement.

The question of James's acquaintance with Bodin's writings themselves is of easy resolution. In his youth, James had in his extensive readings come across Bodin's work.[81] In turn, James was read in France—his *Basilicon Doron* went through three editions in the French translation, and his *Apologia* through at least an equal number.[82] But James's Scottish background and tradition must have made him receptive to the idea of unlimited sovereignty without Bodin's suggestion. In England he merely fell in with the growing trend toward a definition of sovereignty more arbitrarily conceived. His theory was not so foreign to England as might be supposed: there was a growing trend in that direction even during Tudor times.

If Raleigh and Maynwaring as well as Forsett can be called servile agents of the prerogative, what are we to say about the growing pretensions of Parliament on the other hand? Was James's theory of absolute sovereignty so very far removed from that which made the King in Parliament to be "the most sovereign and supreme power above all, and controllable by none"? [83] Here as with James there was no natural law left to guarantee the subjects' property from arbitrary interference.

The monarchy, after all, was not the only institution in the nation to claim absolute sovereignty as opposed to the concept of the constitution which Sir John Fortescue or William Fullbeck advocated. From this point of view it can hardly be claimed that James's political thought was foreign to Eng-

---

[80] N. Kempner, *Raleghs Staatstheoretische Schriften* (Leipzig: Tauchnitz, 1928), p. 32.

[81] W. Kleinecke, *Englische Fuerstenspiegel etc.* (Halle: Niemeyer, 1937), p. 32.

[82] Georges Ascoli, *La Grande-Bretagne devant l'opinion française au XVme siècle* (Paris: Librairie Universitaire, 1930), pp. 2, 14.

[83] Whitelocke's argument in Bates's Case, *State Trials etc.*, II, 483. (Cited incorrectly as Yelverton's argument.)

land.[84] It is true that James with his stubbornness never seems to have realized fully the importance of Parliament as an actual threat to the prerogative. Perhaps this is the reason why he, unlike Elizabeth, failed to secure to the House of Commons the election of influential privy councilors who might guide legislation through Parliament and influence the House. Perhaps, on the other hand, he was sincere when in one of his proclamations he asked for lawful freedom in elections according to the laudable customs of the realm. His personality, it must be admitted, did much to antagonize the Commons but, as we shall see, the advancing claims of Parliament would have been difficult to stem even if King James had been a second Queen Elizabeth. Furthermore, we are apt to remember Elizabeth's glory and to forget the growing dissension between the queen and her Parliaments. After all, both Smith and Hooker wrote during her reign. Interpretations of the great struggle of the English Revolution, under the influence of the historians of the nineteenth century, have tended to be biased in favor of Parliament's claim toward sovereignty. It seems almost as if we could not forgive James for failing to be an earlier edition of Queen Victoria or of King George V.

2

James was the most important advocate, politically, of supreme royal sovereignty. Francis Bacon is usually considered to be "his master's voice." His views on sovereignty are thus doubly interesting in comparison with those of James. It must be said at the outset that with a shrewd and opportunistic politician of Bacon's type, consistency was truly the virtue of small minds. However, a consideration of Bacon in connection with James will serve to remind us that, as yet, a clear-cut concept of sovereignty was not universally accepted. If we started the

[84] This commonplace interpretation of James mars the otherwise excellent paper by George L. Haskins, "Parliament in the Later Middle Ages," *American Historical Review*, LII (1947), 679.

discussion of royalist views of sovereignty with Raleigh, who had grasped its fullest extent, it is fitting that we should conclude it with Bacon, for this devoted servant of the king found himself at the crossroads: in conflict between the traditional ideas, in which as a lawyer he had been trained, and the new quest for sovereignty in the constitution. But with Bacon, too, there emerges finally a sovereign whose limitations are more apparent than real.

"And although the King, in his person, is *solutus legibus*, yet his acts and grants are limited by law and we argue them every day." [85] The king was *solutus legibus*, and yet he was limited, presumably by his own law. Indeed, if the king granted any charter which was repugnant to the maxims, customs, and statutes of the realm, it was *ipso facto* void. [86] The king was ruled and directed by the law, as were his subjects. [87] Moreover, in another place Bacon stated that, while the maxims of the law were the full and perfect conclusions of reason, statute law was the

resolute decrees and absolute judgements of Parliament, established by the King with the common consent of the three estates who do represent the whole and entire body of the realm of England. [88]

All this was not necessarily in conflict with the idea of *solutus legibus*. James had never denied Parliament's part in the making of law, and he professed at least to be directed by these, his own laws. However, Bacon went further in sanctioning parliamentary power than his master ever did. Both held at times the patristic theory of the foundation of governments: the father, Bacon tells us, governs his wife and servants by the prerogatives of sex and providence. The father is the very model of a

[85] Sir Francis Bacon's argument, Case of Post Nati, *State Trials etc.*, II, 580.
[86] Sir Francis Bacon, "Argument on the Charter of Bridewell," *Works of Sir Francis Bacon*, ed. Spedding and Heath (London, 1892), VII, 509-510.
[87] *Ibid.*, p. 509.
[88] *Ibid.*

king. From this James had deduced that the inheritances of his subjects were at his disposal, just as the family's inheritance was the father's to dispose of. But Bacon pursued a different path: to the image of father and family he joined that of the shepherd and his flock. The shepherds were not the owners of the sheep, but it remained their responsibility to feed, care for and govern them.[89]

This trend of Bacon's thought was further advanced when he spoke of a "free monarchy." To James this had meant a monarchy where the monarch had the complete sovereignty, unfettered by the idea of *droit*. But Bacon stated that the constitution of the kingdom appeared to be a free monarchy in nothing better than this: "That there is no land of the subject that is charged to the crown by way of tribute, tax or tallage except it be set by Parliament." [90]

> This is the excellent temper and commixture of this estate, bearing the marks of sovereignty of the king, and of freedom of the subject from tax.[91]

James, too, admitted once before Parliament, as we have seen, that he could not *de jure* tax at will. But he would hardly have admitted, as Bacon did, the chief excellence of a free monarchy to be the freedom of the subjects from arbitrary taxation.

Bacon drew a sharp distinction between the rights of the king and those of the subject. The king had absolute power in war and in making foreign policy. Coinage of money and regulation of foreign trade and commerce were also in his domain.[92]

[89] Bacon in the Case of Post Nati, *State Trials etc.*, II, 578. Contrast Bacon's use of this analogy with that of another more extreme royalist writer. Shepherds, Robert Mockett wrote, may enforce the sheep to suffer the curing of their wounds and compel them to keep in fertile and safe pastures. Robert Mockett, *God and the King* (London, 1615), p. 58.

[90] *Ibid.*

[91] Bacon, "Answer to Sir A. Hay," *Works*, ed. Spedding and Heath (1892), VII, 776-777.

[92] *Ibid.*, "Lowes Case on Tenures," p. 647.

But his ordinary power was limited by law.[93] Here, as opposed to the idea of *legibus solutus*, we seem back in the Tudor tradition.

Baron Fleming had also made a distinction between the king's absolute power for "reason of state" and the ordinary powers in cases of *meum et tuum*, which was limited by law, and could not be changed without Parliament's consent.[94] Coke also held, in tune with the constitutional tradition, that there was a prerogative disputable and a prerogative indisputable. The latter was concerned with such matters as the making of war and peace, the former with questions of *meum et tuum* and was bounded by law.[95] "God forbid," ejaculated Bacon, "the king should determine the right of the subject; for whensoever the law gives the subject a right, it giveth a remedy in open court legally." [96]

The king could grant no new office where prescription was alleged.[97] The law favored those who had ancient rights: "Right cannot die," said Bacon, quoting Littleton.[98] The law was thus "the highest inheritance the king has." [99] But here the law seems to be more than just the inheritance of the king, in the sense that the king may do with it as he pleases. Bacon's view of Magna Carta comes close to a belief in fundamental law—and here at least he is very close to his great rival, Chief Justice Coke. The idea that a right never dies puts that right outside of the king's reach. Bacon declared the Charter of Bridewell invalid because it conflicted with Article 29 of Magna Carta, by which no free man should be imprisoned save by the law of the land.[100] Indeed, Bacon went so far as to say:

[93] *Ibid.*, p. 778.
[94] Fleming in Bates's Case, *State Trials etc.*, II, 389-392.
[95] *Commons Debates*, 1621, ed. Notestein, Relf, Simpson, IV, 79.
[96] Bacon, "De Rege Inconsulto," *Works*, ed. Spedding and Heath (1892), VII, 697.
[97] *Ibid.*, p. 716.
[98] Bacon, "Reading on the Statute of Uses," *ibid.*, p. 421.
[99] Bacon, "Argument on the Commission of Bridewell," *ibid.*, p. 509.
[100] *Ibid.*, p. 512.

... Ye see it very plainly that neither procurement nor act done either by the king or any other person, or any act of Parliament or other thing may in any ways alter or change any one point contained in the said great Charter of England.[101]

Altogether, the law favored life, liberty, and dower, because it was in this respect grounded on the law of nature.[102]

The king was *legibus solutus*—yet he was limited by a law which seemed to have a position of quasi-independence from the king. Perhaps Bacon's idea as to the position of that law was best expressed in a passage from his argument in the case of the Post Nati:

> Law no doubt is the great organ by which sovereign power does move, and may be truly compared to the sinews in a natural body, as the sovereignty may be compared to the spirits: for if sinews be without the spirits, they are dead and without motion . . . so the laws without the king's power, are dead; the king's power, except the laws be corroborated will never move constantly, but be full of staggering and trepidation.[103]

The king was here a vital part in the existence of the law. To Smith, Morice, and Hooker he had also been a vital part in the legal process. But to Bacon corroboration of the law was not based on grounds of superior law, or even on grounds of constitutional principles. It was grounded rather on utility, an argument similar to Raleigh's. And yet in matters of *meum et tuum* the law must apparently have a measure of independence from the king.

Bacon then seemed not really to share the view with James that the king was completely *legibus solutus*. He did, at times at least, not try to whittle away the common law, though the sovereignty was part of its main ingredient. However, Bacon's emphasis on the absolute power of the king as superior in the last resort to his ordinary powers came near to making the king

---

[101] *Ibid.*, p. 513.

[102] "Reading on the Statute of Uses," *ibid.*, p. 421.

[103] Bacon, Case of the Post Nati, *State Trials etc.*, II, 580.

legibus solutus in spite of his other professions of regard for the independence of the common law. If a case involved the king, it could not be disputed without consulting the king himself. His rights could not be disputed among private persons.[104] The king, here at least, was without the law.

Presumably, then, the king would be a judge in his own cases, a view James, in believing himself the last court of appeal, would have shared, and a view which common lawyers like Coke vigorously opposed. Even when a common lawyer held that the king was the "principal conservator of the peace, *capitalis justiciarius Angliae*," he would hasten to add that the king could personally sit in judgment *except* in cases to which he was a party.[105] The king, in Bacon's view, could not interfere with matters of *meum et tuum* directly, but he was himself above all legal restraints, inferior to none, not even to the law.

Moreover, with Bacon, where the good of the commonwealth was concerned, "necessity privilegeth not," as we saw above. Here again the idea of reason of state tended to nullify all rights of the subject, despite professions of their sacredness from royal interference. How should it be otherwise when the king alone could determine an emergency, when in this case no natural law protected the subject's property? It need not astonish us to see Bacon dwelling on the importance of reason of state, for had he not publicly avowed his indebtedness to Machiavelli? [106] It is equally probable that he was acquainted

---

[104] Bacon, "De Rege Inconsulto," *Works,* ed. Spedding and Heath (1892), VII, 690. See also Bacon, "Charge against Mr. Whitelocke," *Works,* ed. Montagu (1827), VII, 384-385.

[105] Bacon, "Maxims of the Law," *Works,* ed. Spedding and Heath (1892), VII, 346.

[106] N. Kempner, *Raleghs Staatstheoretische Schriften* (Leipzig: Tauchnitz, 1928), p. 23. Typically enough Bacon equated the Machiavellian term "policy" with the science of "civil knowledge." Napoleone Orsini, "Policy, or Language of Elizabethan Machiavellianism," *Journal of the Warburg and Courtauld Institutes,* IX (1946), 123. It is extremely probable that Bacon was also acquainted with Bodin. One source through which he could have gotten the Frenchman's definition of sovereignty was Pierre Charron's *Of Wisdom* (London, 1612). Napoleone Orsini, *Bacone e Machiavelli* (Genoa: E. Degli Orfini, 1936), p. 197.

with Jean Bodin, perhaps through Pierre Charron's *Of Wisdom*.

Bacon's views on the position of the judges, which were also the views of James, moreover, were dangerous because they removed the last security which the common law possessed against arbitrary might. Not only were judges to Bacon "lions under the throne," but before the idea of reason of state all independence of procedure and custom also had to give way.[107] Questions of estate concerning thousands of lives were more important than was the individual life or inheritance.[108]

Bacon might thus say that the king in his person was *legibus solutus,* and yet was limited by the law, that his charters, if contrary to the law of the realm, were void, that no one according to Magna Carta should be imprisoned arbitrarily. Yet in the last resort the king was above the law in his person, and the corroboration of law by Parliament was merely a thing useful and good. But reason of state was a bigger thing than mere individual rights, and moreover, judges were nothing but the king's pawns. Surely here the quasi-independence of the common law was a feeble thing. Indeed, it was just as feeble as Forsett's limitations on the king, who limited himself by his own free will. Bacon might say that while the king was directed by his law just as his subjects were, yet he was nevertheless outside its reach, by virtue of his office.

It should be pointed out again, however, that Bacon was much less single-minded in his views of sovereignty than was James. England was a free monarchy for its people could be taxed only by Parliament; English law was based partly on natural law favoring "life, liberty and dower."

Bacon, too, in a manner of speaking, was at the crossroads,

---

[107] Bacon, "Speech on taking his Place in Chancery," *Works,* ed. Montagu (1827), VII, 251.

[108] Peacham's Case, *State Trials etc.,* II, 873. Here it should again be emphasized that Bacon always held theoretically to the division of law into *ius publicum,* "the sinews of the Commonwealth," and *ius privatum.* "Preparation towards the Union of Laws," *Works,* ed. Spedding and Heath (1892), VII, 731.

trained as he was in the Elizabethan school of statecraft, serving as he did a monarch who held the absolute view of sovereignty. We know that Bacon the scientist had an abiding love for facts as opposed to the idols of the market place. Perhaps he was trying to square the legal facts, as he had learned them at the Inns of Court, with the fact of royal sovereignty which he was learning from his royal master, James I. His ideas were thus full of contradictions, never worked out so fully and systematically as were, for example, those of Raleigh.

While Bacon can be said to have been at the crossroads, in other writers we have seen a considerable development of the idea of sovereignty into a clear dictum of complete royal control. Forsett, Raleigh, Maynwaring, and James all stressed the idea of sovereignty and minimized the idea of *droit*. Even where the old concept of the king's sphere of power and the people's sphere of rights was still intact, the idea of reason of state went far to destroy its reality, for there was little talk about the medieval natural law and much about the king's large emergency powers. If there was a law of God or nature, its main function seems to have been to guarantee the sovereignty of the ruler, not the rights of the subject. Seneca's statement, "To the king authority over all, to private persons property," seems to have lost its meaning, for the sinews of the commonwealth, the law, was no longer removed from human interference so far as the royalist writers were concerned. Judges were inferior magistrates; Parliament was a subaltern court beneath the king.

The ideas of men like James and Bacon did not spring up without cause. We have seen how there had been changes in the Tudor tradition on which English writers could build their ideas of sovereignty. Jean Bodin's fate seems to have been similar in England to what it was in France. Here too sovereignty was enhanced, while the element of *droit* tended to be more and more ignored. Neither James's nor Bacon's ideas can be linked closely to the Frenchman's formulation of sovereignty.

Even if Jean Bodin had not put his formula at the disposal of English writers, the quest for sovereignty would have taken its course.

This will become still clearer when we turn to consider Parliament's idea of sovereignty.

V

THE SOVEREIGNTY OF PARLIAMENT

I

PARLIAMENT, AS WELL AS THE ROYALISTS, joined in the search for a final authority in the state. Too often, however, the idea of parliamentary sovereignty has been conceived as the ultimate power of Parliament alone—*i.e.*, without the king as a vital part.[1] The idea of parliamentary sovereignty first arose, however, as the concept of the sovereignty of the King in Parliament.

It thus fastens onto the tradition of Sir Thomas Smith. By 1628 one pamphleteer stated that the Great Court of Parliament

is so far removed from my sight, that I cannot presume a certain representation with these weak species of eyeing those mysteries: I make bold by way of explanation, introduction and deduction of Sir Thomas Smith's Commonwealth to deliver this only:

[1] F. D. Wormuth gives this impression when he stresses that according to the Long Parliament it was now the representative body of the kingdom and charged with a trust on its behalf. "Not the law, but the kingdom, is now the object of concern; and Parliamentary sovereignty lacks only avowal." *The Royal Prerogative, 1603–1649* (Ithaca: Cornell University Press, 1939), p. 109.

and he went on to cite Smith's list of parliamentary powers, concluding that the "authority of it is absolute and bindeth all manner of persons." [2] By 1628 Smith would have been shocked to see to what lengths parliamentary claims had gone. By that time even matters which Smith had put under the governance of the king alone had come under the sole purview of Parliament, "the reformer of the Commonwealth." [3]

The most complete statement of the sovereignty of the King in Parliament came from Whitelocke, fully eighteen years before the pamphleteer wrote his lines and quoted from Sir Thomas Smith. Whitelocke stated his position in Bodinian terms. Arguing the case of the king's right to levy taxes upon imports in the case of Bates in 1606, Whitelocke stated that where the sovereign power lay in the kingdom, there was the right of imposition. He then set out to find the sovereign power in the commonwealth. He agreed that this power was in the king, but the king himself had a twofold power, one in Parliament, "he is assisted with the consent of the whole state," and one out of Parliament, "as he is sole and singular guided merely by his own will." Of these two powers one is greater than the other, and can correct and control the other, "which sovereign power is *potestas suprema,* a power that can control all other powers, and cannot be controlled but by itself." [4]

On behalf of the king, Baron Fleming had submitted a somewhat similar plea. But Fleming had never claimed any one power of the king to be supreme over any other. He may have implied that the extraordinary power of the king was more perfect than the ordinary, but he did not indulge in a conscious search for the sovereign power in the state.[5]

[2] Thomas Powell, *The Attourney's Academy etc.* (London, 1628), pp. 218, 219.

[3] *Parliamentary Debates,* 1625, ed. S. R. Gardiner (Camden Society, 1873), p. 82.

[4] *State Trials etc.,* ed. T. Howell (London, 1809), II, 482. The speech is here ascribed to Yelverton; Gardiner thinks Whitelocke made the speech and he seems to be correct, for Yelverton was far from being an opponent of the king, *Parliamentary Debates,* 1610 ed., S. R. Gardiner, (Camden Society, 1862), p. 85, fn. d.

[5] For Fleming's argument, *vide supra,* chap. iii.

Whitelocke, however, proceeded to prove that the king was sovereign in his Parliament. Here Whitelocke, like Bodin before him, associated the idea of sovereignty with the characteristic of lawmaking. No man ever read that the king made laws without Parliament; therefore th emaking of law in Parliament "is the original right of the kingdom, and the very natural constitution of our state and policy, being one of the highest rights of sovereign power." [6] And levying impositions was a change in the law. To prove his contentions he cited Sir John Fortescue, who had said that "England is *principatus mixtus et politicus*, the King has his sovereign power in Parliament...." [7] Here truly we have an old idea stated in a new reference. Did the *principatus mixtus et politicus* denote to Fortescue that the king had his sovereign power in Parliament? Certainly not in the way in which Whitelocke used the word "sovereignty." The very idea of a *potestas suprema* in the state was foreign to the medieval way of thought. Whitelocke's statement that the power of Parliament "maketh it the most sovereign and supreme power above all and controllable by none" [8] would have made no sense to Fortescue, who was still within the bonds of natural and divine law, and for whom this search for a supreme power in the state would have been devoid of meaning.

Whitelocke went on to demonstrate the practical supremacy of Parliament. The king alone had no right to change the possession of property, but if the king did this in Parliament, it was a different matter, for that which was done in Parliament was "Assisted and strengthened by the consent of the whole Kingdom." [9] Previously Smith and Hooker had held this idea of law as deriving from popular belief expressed through a representative Parliament, and it was constantly restated throughout the first half of the seventeenth century.

It is fit and just, that every man doth join in making that which shall bind and govern him; and because every man cannot be per-

[6] *State Trials etc.*, II, 483.
[7] *Ibid.*, p. 486.
[8] *Ibid.*, p. 483.
[9] *Ibid.*, p. 486.

sonally present, therefore a representative body is made to perform that service.[10]

Here was one of the props for Parliament's claims. Coke might wish that Parliament would confine itself to public issues and not interfere with the *meum et tuum*, but what in the end was to stop the people from binding themselves? [11] Moreover, the idea of representation could also be used against the House of Lords, for the Lords represented only themselves, but in the Commons every man was at least the representative of a whole county or a borough.[12] By 1626 we find the king referring to Parliament as the "representative body of the whole kingdom, and the great counsel of the realm." [13]

It is on this theory of representation that much of Parliament's claim to power was based, shading over as it did into the idea of Parliament as the custodian of the "common good." Once the force of supernatural laws guaranteeing property was gone, what was to stop the Parliament from interfering with each man's property in the name of "representation"? Two years before Whitelocke argued the case of Bates, Parliament had already taken pains to assert, in the Apology of 1604, that the voice of the people, in things of their knowledge, might be likened to the voice of God. Whitelocke here held a theory which seems to have become fairly commonplace among his contemporaries. The parallel to Smith's thought is clear. He too believed that the King in Parliament could change property rights because all men were represented in Parliament. On the other hand, not only was Whitelocke far removed from Fortescue's *dominium politicum et regale;* he was even a step beyond Sir Thomas Smith. Smith never consciously stated that

---

[10] *Parliamentary Diary of Robert Bowyer,* ed. D. H. Willson (Minneapolis: University of Minnesota Press, 1931), p. 259.

[11] *E.g.,* Sir Edward Coke, *Fourth Institutes* (London, 1797), chap. i; also *Second Institutes* (London, 1797), Pt. I, pp. 73 ff.

[12] *Parliamentary Diary of Robert Bowyer,* p. 234.

[13] *A Declaration of the true cause which moved his Majesty to assemble and dissolve the Parliament* (London, 1626), p. 15. For a similar expression: *Royal Proclamation,* 14 August, 1625.

the King in Parliament was the sovereign "controllable by none."

It seems possible, therefore, to say that with Whitelocke we possess a clear statement of the doctrine of parliamentary sovereignty, always remembering that we have here the sovereignty of the King in Parliament and not that of Parliament without the king.

Even Whitelocke, however, left to the king certain rights which he could exercise outside of Parliament—above all, the right over foreign policy and over coinage.[14] But, on the other hand, the sovereign power in Parliament included, besides the making of law, both naturalization and the highest appeal in judicial matters.[15]

Whitelocke's assertions were not to remain merely the random opinions of a member of Parliament; they were to be officially adopted by the House of Commons four years later in the Apology of 1610:

> The policy and constitution of this, your kingdom, appropriates unto the kings of the realm, with the assent of the Parliament, as well the sovereign power of making laws, as that of taxing, or imposing upon the subjects goods or merchandises, wherein they have justly such a propriety as may not without their consent be altered or changed.[16]

Here are propounded both the concept of sovereign power as linked to the making of law and the idea of representation.

The claim to sovereignty as lodged in the King in Parliament seems then to have been formulated by 1610. That same year James was to reject the one solution which might have staved off the growing conflict between himself and Parliament. The Great Contract, by providing the king with a stable revenue, would have freed the country from much taxation. James would have become the pensioner of Parliament. In rejecting the Contract, James was apparently influenced by a paper of Sir Julius

[14] *State Trials etc.*, II, 483.
[15] *Ibid.*
[16] *Ibid.*, p. 521.

Caesar. Caesar held up before James the disgrace of a king's selling his prerogatives for money—lawful prerogatives which his ancestors on the throne had thought never to part with.[17] Such an argument was certain to have a telling effect on James. When as a consequence he began to stiffen in his demands, the Contract was bound to fail. At last, early in the next year, James dissolved his first Parliament. Henceforth the conflict was clearly inevitable.

However, even if we date the irreparable breach between the king and Parliament from 1610, the ideological battle lines had been formed earlier. James's theories had undergone their slight adjustment to English conditions by that date. They were not going to modify before the pretensions of Parliament. Consent had nothing to do with his power over his subjects' lands and goods, for was he not the "father of his people"? The king was *legibus solutus;* Parliament's assent was a favor which the king graciously granted of his own free will. Had he not countered the Commons' claims that their privileges were their birthright with the counterassertion that they were derived "from him and by his grant" [18]—and this only one year after he came to the throne? Had the Commons, in its turn, not included in its Apology of 1604, passed in James's first Parliament, a singular passage explaining its relative tractability in the reign of Elizabeth as due to the regard for her sex and age? Thus even two years before Whitelocke spoke, the Commons had clearly implied that its "care to avoid all trouble" was past, a claim which sounds all the more remarkable if we remember the stormy Parliaments of the last years of the queen. By 1610 both sides were beginning to push to their ultimate extent their conscious search for a sovereign authority in the state.

It is difficult to prove that either Whitelocke or the men who framed the Petition of 1610 were familiar with Jean Bodin. But their ideas were certainly couched in Bodinian terminology.

[17] *Parliamentary Debates,* 1610, ed. S. R. Gardiner (Camden Society, 1862), App. D, p. 175.

[18] Sir G. Prothero, *Select Statutes etc.* (Oxford: Oxford University Press, 1913), p. 326. James re-echoed this sentiment in 1621, *ibid.,* p. 313.

Yet these assertions of parliamentary sovereignty may be said in a manner to fasten onto the Tudor tradition.

2

The views of men like Whitelocke did not spring up without cause. It is here that we must remain closer to the chronological development and the practical motivations than in our previous analysis of the royalist quest for sovereignty. For we are now concerned with a corporate body of people rather than with outstanding individuals through whose thought we have been able to illustrate the developments up to this point.

Religious and economic reasons, as well as a realization of the political developments on the continent of Europe, spurred on Parliament's quest for sovereignty almost in spite of itself. Only in this context can we understand Parliament's struggle for sovereignty. The most important considerations were no doubt the economic ones related to Parliament's sovereign claims over property, but the religious issue played its rôle hand in hand with the economic.

It is difficult to ascertain when the religious and economic opposition to the crown fused in Parliament, but it was popularly said that James's first Parliament was already three parts Puritan.[19] By 1611 the Commons seems to have wanted a complete change in the ecclesiastical government.[20] In 1621 Pym would answer the charge that a Puritan clique had pushed through the House a bill for the better observation of the Sabbath by contending that the Puritans could not have occasioned the bill as it had been passed by the whole House.[21]

That same year, 1621, poor Mr. Shepherd found himself sequestered from the House of Commons for pointing out that the Puritan Sabbath really equaled the Jewish Saturday and for

[19] S. R. Gardiner, *History of England 1603–1642* (London: Longmans, Green & Co., 1883), I, 78.

[20] *Ibid.*, II, 85.

[21] *Commons Debates, 1621*, ed. Notestein, Relf, Simpson (New Haven: Yale University Press, 1935), II, 95.

directly accusing the Commons of not making so much as a "mouse-trap" for the Puritans while it laid nothing but "snares" for the papists.[22] Moreover, the juxtaposition of religious and economic elements in the Commons' supports for the Protestants in the Thirty Years War, to which we shall recur, is important, for it shows conclusively that by 1621 Parliament was profoundly imbued with the quest for economic power as well as with Puritanism.

Indeed, Puritanism was well fitted to push Parliament along the road toward opposition to the monarchy and to bolster the parliamentary quest for sovereignty. Even Queen Elizabeth had had to deal with the rising tide of Puritanism, as well as with the economic pressure against royal controls. For example, in 1580 the House, by a majority of fifteen votes, resolved for a fast in spite of the queen's "mislike" for this action, which impugned her authority in matters ecclesiastical.[23] But Elizabeth was inclined to give way before pressure on the part of Parliament.

Here, too, James's stubbornness came into play. He had his fill of Puritanism in Scotland. He would have difficulty in forgetting Melville, who one day had plucked him by the sleeve and loudly proclaimed, "Jesus [is] the King of the Church whose subject James VI is and of whose kingdom he is not a king . . . but a member." [24] He must have shuddered when he heard that Wentworth had exclaimed in his English Parliament in 1610, ". . . the King is subject to another King and we all pray *veniat regnum tuum.*" [25] No wonder that James did not look with favor on the Millenary Petition, moderate though its demands might have been. To James, the idea of "No Bishop, no King" was a perfectly defensible one. Did the Puritan min-

[22] *Ibid.,* p. 82.

[23] Sir Simon D'Ewes, *Journal of all the Parliaments etc.* (London, 1682), pp. 238, 285.

[24] *The Political Works of James I,* ed. C. H. McIlwain (Cambridge: Harvard University Press, 1918), p. xxi.

[25] *Parliamentary Debates,* 1610, ed. Gardiner (1862), p. 61.

isters not intend to reform the Established Church to make it "agreeable to the example of other reformed churches?"[26]

It must not be forgotten that James and Archbishop Bancroft did make an attempt to obtain a better ministry. They introduced a bill into the House extending the tithe and increasing appropriations by means of parliamentary subsidy. They realized that without better pay there would not be a better and more learned ministry. The House rejected the bill.[27] Perhaps Parliament's purse and Parliament's soul were in conflict here, and the purse won. Or, more probably, the House was not interested in having the king reform "his" Church, but wanted nothing less than a church of its own reformation. At any rate, we have an obvious impasse between king and Parliament. Gardiner holds that by 1611 the Commons wanted nothing less than a complete change in ecclesiastical government.[28] One year before this, it is well to remember, the Great Contract, that pensioning of the king which might have staved off the economic conflict, had failed.

James himself tried to steer a middle course in matters of religion. Thus in 1622 he admonished all preachers "not to presume causelessly to fall into invectives against persons either Papists or Puritans."[29] Yet he had issued in 1617 the challenging declaration against the "Sabbath" which he was to embody later in his *Book of Sports*.[30] On the other hand his vacillating policy against the Catholics and his dealings with Spain gave the Puritans much concern. Perhaps nothing shows the Commons' attitude on religious questions more clearly than does the fact

[26] From a subscription sent to the ministers before the convocation of the Hampton Court conference. W. H. Frere, *A History of the English Church in the Reigns of Elizabeth and James I* (London: Macmillan, 1904), p. 294. The identical sentence was inserted in 1643 in the Solemn League and Covenant. At that time it was taken to mean the Presbyterian Church of Scotland.

[27] *Ibid.*, p. 332.

[28] Gardiner, *History of England*, II, 85.

[29] Prothero, *Select Statutes etc.*, p. 432, art. V.

[30] J. R. Tanner, *Constitutional Conflicts in Seventeenth Century England* (Cambridge: Cambridge University Press, 1948), p. 15.

that communion became compulsory for all members of the House.[31] Not only this, but in 1614, for example, the Commons avoided Westminster Abbey for fear of "popish" customs in the taking of the communion.[32] Thus did the Commons assert their militant Protestantism in the face of a monarchy which seemed tainted with Romanism. However, in their quest for a change of religion to suit their aims, Parliament had to tread warily. As late as 1621 Sir Edwin Sandys had to affirm that a king might alter religion when he pleased, for this had been affirmed by the Bill of 35 Elizabeth. "If hereafter the King turn to be a Papist then we must call the Protestants Papists." [33] How the House must have winced at this remark. Such fears must have incited the Puritans against the crown.

The religious element alone might have been sufficient to spur Parliament on to action, but the religious went hand in hand with the economic. Concerning Spain the Commons on the one hand asserted that there was no halting between the two religions, and on the other hand beheld with evident delight the riches of the Indies which might be conquered for the advancement and glory of England's trade. In 1628 Mr. Rouse used the Biblical story of Job to link true religion and the sacredness of private property. "It was an old trick of the devil," he told the Commons, "when he meant to take away Job's Religion, he begins at his Goods. . . . But let us do as Job did, he held fast his Religion, and then his Goods were restor'd to him with Advantage; and if we hold fast to our Religion these things shall be added unto us." [34] To fight for the true religion here meant a promise of added profit on earth. Mr. Rouse's reading of Job may serve as an example of how closely the economic and re-

[31] On February 5, 1621, for example, the motion that all of the House might take the Communion was made on the grounds (among others) that it would be a means to know the faith of those in the House. *Commons Debates*, 1621, ed. Notestein, Relf, Simpson, IV, 11.

[32] This incident is told in Tanner, *Constitutional Conflicts*, p. 31.

[33] *Commons Debates*, 1621, ed. Notestein, Relf, Simpson, II, 285.

[34] *The Proceedings and Debates of the House of Commons etc.*, collected by Sir Thomas Crewe (London, 1707), pp. 16, 17.

ligious motives were linked in the minds of many of the king's opponents.

Besides the economic and religious incentive to parliamentary supremacy, there seems however to have been another thought in the minds of the members of Parliament which deserves mention. They seemed to have been aware of the trend of affairs on the continent of Europe. We have already cited Sir Thomas Overbury's observations; [35] another traveler, Robert Dallington, joined in pointing out the absolutism of the French monarchy. [36] A manuscript translation of Bodin's *République* pointed out that the prince was an absolute sovereign in the "True Monarchies" of France, Spain, England, and other states. In these "True Monarchies" sovereignty was an absolute power not subject to any law. Moreover, on the title page of this translation Bodin was called a Protestant according to the church of Geneva. [37] Thus a Calvinist writer himself was made to point out the similarities of all "True Monarchies." Such a view must have been frightening to the Puritans as well as to Parliament as a whole, which did not believe in such a dangerous equation between English and European forms of government.

Thus Sir Robert Phillips cried out that "we are the last monarchy in Christendom to retain our original rights and constitutions." [38] To the charge that impositions were levied in France and Spain, Parliament replied that they were rather *de facto* than *de jure* in those countries, for these nations had never had parliaments or assemblies. [39] With acute historical understanding one member of Parliament pointed out that subsidies might grow into a stable revenue, and that this had occurred in

[35] *Vide supra*, pp. 30, 31.

[36] Robert Dallington, *Method for Travel etc.* (London, n.d.).

[37] *Discourse of Jean Bodin*, British Museum, Harl. 6867, fol. 253. It is difficult to date this translation; it is listed in the British Museum under the reign of James I.

[38] *Parliamentary Debates*, 1625, ed. Gardiner (1873), p. 110.

[39] *Court and Times of James I*, ed. Thomas Birch (London, 1849), p. 1. John Chamberlain to Sir Dudley Carleton, May 26, 1614, p. 312. Sandys spoke to this point, as well as Thomas Wentworth. Wentworth cited the loss of the Netherlands as due to the impositions imposed by Spain, p. 312.

Spain and Naples, where these taxes had started as voluntary contributions and were "now made certain and due." [40]

This awareness of European developments on the part of members of Parliament had its counterpart in the equal awareness of these developments by royalist writers. England, so one writer asserted, is a monarchy like France and Spain, "wherein one is sovereign as the head." [41] We have observed that John Cowell made the statement that the king of England is endowed with the same regalities as the most absolute prince in the world might possess. Raleigh, in his turn, had asserted that England as a monarchy was on the same plane with France.[42]

While royalist writers were thus stressing the similarities between England and the monarchies of Europe, Parliament men naturally sought to combat a comparison so dangerous to their liberties. At times royalists were even prone to use the state of Europe as a threat to an intransigent Parliament. Thus, when the Commons was about to impeach the Duke of Buckingham, the Vice Chamberlain warned the House "that the King will never take new counsels, whilst we do that here, which is *dignum nobis*. The like Parliament, as ours, in other countries, yet all abandoned but here. . . ." [43] Such veiled threats must only have served to make Parliament still more resentful of comparisons between the state of Europe and that of England, although it must be added that Bacon used the federalism of Spain to sway Parliament for the union between Scotland and England.[44]

On behalf of Parliament, Attorney Hobart replied frankly to the royalists that if all *Jura Majestatis* be incident to a king,

[40] *Parliamentary Debates*, 1625, ed. Gardiner (1873), p. 125.

[41] William Loe, *Vox Clamantis etc.* (London, 1621), pp. 38, 39. Another writer, arguing anonymously for the Union of England and Scotland, cited the natural frontiers of France and Spain: "The Montes, Perrenai, the Sea, the Alpes," as examples which nature herself had appointed, for England and Scotland together rounded out the natural frontiers of the island of Britain. *Rapta Tatio etc.* (London, 1604).

[42] *Vide supra*, p. 43.

[43] *Journal of the House of Commons*, I, 12 May, 1626, p. 860.

[44] *Ibid.*, III, 19 April, 1604, p. 950.

then all kings possess them. But the king of England "has not all of these." He went on to cite Fortescue and Sir Thomas Smith on the limitations of the king of England.[45] Perhaps this issue is best summed up by the controversy between Watton and Sir Roger Owen in 1614. Watton had made the distinction between "elective kings," who are dependent on the will of the people and who may not impose without consent, and hereditary kings, who are not so bound. To this Sir Roger Owen replied that this issue was not to be decided "upon histories as upon the ancient laws of England which must only decide the question." [46] Parliamentary men wanted no parallels drawn between the monarchs of Europe and their own king. They seem to have been aware of the trend toward absolutism in Europe—though even here at times, when it suited their purpose, the Commons could invoke the European example.[47]

We have indicated somewhat the religious feeling and the reaction to European developments as stimuli to Parliament's quest for sovereignty. However, the economic stimulus was by far the most significant. Parliament as adjudicator and protector of property rights presented, surely, the most fundamental issue between the king and his Parliaments. We have seen already how Parliament's growing jurisdiction over property rights, based on the waning power of natural law, was one of the chief elements of change in the Tudor constitution. It is this development which we must consider further.

John U. Nef has shown that there were two distinct industrial revolutions in England, not one alone. The first of these rapid economic changes occurred in the century which began with the dissolution of the monasteries and ended with the outbreak of the Civil War.[48]

Is it merely coincidental that this period spans the gaining

---

[45] *Parliamentary Debates,* 1610, ed. Gardiner (1862), pp. 90, 118.

[46] *Commons Debates,* 1621, ed. Notestein, Relf, Simpson, VII, 644.

[47] Thus Pym cited precedents of other states, as well as parliamentary examples, to the effect that dangerous books should be suppressed: *Journal of the House of Commons,* I, 17 April, 1626, p. 845.

[48] John U. Nef, *Industry and Government in France and England, 1540–1640* (Philadelphia: The American Philosophical Society, 1940), p. 1.

of the initiative by the House of Commons? It seems hardly necessary to point out that Parliament's attacks on such restrictive economic practices as monopolies were linked with the growing prosperity of the English merchant classes. The cry for freedom of trade was constantly heard. Its advocacy was the common ground between men as far apart in their thinking as Coke and Bacon.[49] In 1605, for example, Fuller beat a speedy retreat when he found himself opposed by the governor of the merchant adventurers over a bill for the true making and dressing of woolen cloth which was thought to be restrictive in nature.[50] The quest for free trade went to great lengths. Even the merchant adventurers found themselves subject to an investigation by Parliament because of monopolistic practices. Indeed, in 1624, their monopoly was severely curtailed.[51]

The debate on the act against usury in 1624 may serve as an added indication of the spirit of the men who now "represented" their fellow countrymen in the Commons. Usury had, of course, been regarded with abhorrence by the men of the middle ages. Throughout the sixteenth century, however, ideas concerning it had undergone profound modifications. By 1571 the exaction of interest ceased to be a criminal offense, providing that the interest did not exceed ten per cent.[52]

The Usury Act of 1624 as passed by the Commons did not modify this concept to any great extent. The significant thing, however, was the opposition this act encountered on the floor of the House. Bateman's speech might have been typical of the new practical attitude towards usury. The "labour of the House has been to increase Trade, and usury legislation might have the opposite effect. . . . Money in Spain and Italy at a higher rate. All our Moneys will be carried thither." [53] Here was the

[49] Coke, *Fourth Institutes*, p. 31, and *Second Institutes*, pt. I, 47. Sir Francis Bacon, "Reading on the Statute of Uses," *Works of Sir Francis Bacon*, ed. Spedding and Heath (London, 1892), VII, 425.

[50] *Parliamentary Diary of Robert Bowyer*, pp. 33, 34.

[51] *Journal of the House of Commons*, I, 10 May, 1624, p. 787.

[52] R. H. Tawney, *Religion and the Rise of Capitalism* (New York: Harcourt, 1926), p. 180.

[53] *Journal of the House of Commons*, I, 26 April, 1624, p. 775. A similar

hardheaded merchant speaking, to whom the system of ethics inherited from the middle ages was less important than was the state of England's trade. Yet there were others who found the Statute of Usury difficult to reconcile with the laws and ordinances of God, which must be kept inviolable. There are men, writes the lawyer, Rastell, in his *Exposition* (which went through sixteen editions between 1592 and 1639), who gather that because of the statute they may take interest with a good conscience.

But rather let such think that that statute was made upon the like cause that moved Moses to give a bill of divorce to the Israelites, as namely to avoid greater mischief, and for the hardness of their hearts.[54]

Perhaps the opposition against all usury legislation because of its harmfulness to trade was a part of the discarding of God's law and of medieval ideas of the law of nature, which might also block the way to a full parliamentary sovereignty. To Sir Edward Coke, typically enough, usury was still against the laws both of God and of nature.[55]

Usury legislation, in the opinion of many Parliament men, would conflict with the principles involved in "An Act for Free Trade into all Countries," which had its first reading the preceding year,[56] or with an act for "Free trade in Welsh cloth," which was passed into law the same year as was the Statute of Usury.[57] Indeed, in 1621 a bill for the restraint of Welsh cloth was jettisoned by the House because it was said to be against the common liberty of the subject.[58] In that same year another

statement, though not as blunt, made in the debates on usury in 1571 is quoted in Benjamin N. Nelson, *The Idea of Usury* (Princeton: Princeton University Press, 1949), p. 84.

[54] John Rastell, *An Exposition of Certain Difficult and Obscure Words and Terms of the Laws of this Realm etc.* (London, 1592), pp. 192, 193.

[55] Sir Edward Coke, *Third Institutes* (London, 1797), p. 152.

[56] *Journal of the House of Commons*, I, 25 March, 1623, p. 749.

[57] *Journal of the House of Commons*, I, 7 April, 1624, p. 757.

[58] *Commons Debates*, 1621, ed. Notestein, Relf, Simpson, IV, 95. Another instance of an indignant rejection of a bill regulating cloth manufacturing is found in *Parliamentary Diary of Robert Bowyer*, p. 12.

bill for free trade into all countries was introduced into the House.[59] Sir Edward Coke himself, influenced by contemporary economic ambitions, listed among the matters most hurtful to the commonwealth the creation of new monopolistic corporations which trade in foreign parts and at home, because they tend to hinder trade and traffic.[60]

Perhaps Justice Dalton best expressed the feeling of the times. No man, he wrote, shall be restrained from practicing a lawful trade, for law "abhorreth idleness as the mother of all evil." "So that without an act of Parliament no man may be restrained, either to work in any lawful trade, or to use divers mysteries or trades. . . ." [61] Coke, too, voiced similar sentiments when he included in his definition of the liberty of Englishmen the right of any man to have his clothes dressed where he will. Therefore he declared an ordinance by the merchant tailors, telling the people where their clothes should be dressed, null and void.[62] He went on, typically enough, to quote Darcy's case, where monopolies had been declared illegal at common law.

It was only natural that the urge toward free trade in an expanding economic society should find its expression in Parliament. It tried to pension the king through the Great Contract and thus minimize his taxation and commercial exactions. On the same rock, for example, James's much-hoped-for union between England and Scotland floundered. Member after member of Parliament rose from his seat and accused the Scots of monopolistic practices. Had they not got the trade with Dieppe solely into their hands? [63] The Scotch merchants had bribed the French in order to conceal their true advantages in that country.[64] Twice the Commons called committees of

---

[59] *Commons Debates*, 1621, ed. Notestein, Relf, Simpson, IV, 272. It did not pass because it "seemed to limit the King's prerogative in making Corporations." *Ibid.*, IV, 273.

[60] Coke, *Second Institutes*, pt. I, 47.

[61] Michael Dalton, *The Justice of the Peace etc.* (London, 1728), p. 182.

[62] Coke, *Second Institutes*, pt. I, 47.

[63] *Parliamentary Diary of Robert Bowyer*, p. 265, (n. 1).

[64] *Ibid.*, p. 265.

prominent merchants to the bar in order to testify on the effect of the proposed union.[65] It was largely because of the commercial opposition that the whole matter was finally dropped.[66]

3

The economic desires of those in Parliament went hand in hand with the religious quest and the fear of following European examples. It was only to be expected that on these issues Parliament would clash with the monarchy. James, as we have seen, was no Puritan in religion, and economically the idea of "free trade," if enforced, would rob him of a great part of his income, which was derived from customs, duties, and monopolies. The economic aspect of the dispute between king and Commons acted as a great stimulant to Parliament's claims over property.

To Coke, the liberty of Englishmen included the right of any man to have his clothes dressed where he would. But what if Parliament itself, claiming sole authority over property, interfered with that liberty? What if Parliament in turn should restrict property in a monopolistic sense? The answer to this question, bound up with Coke's attitude toward Parliament's power and more specifically with the gradual recognition by the courts of Parliament's control over property, will shed much light on this vital area of Parliament's quest for sovereignty and control.

Justice Dalton had allowed an act of Parliament the authority, indeed the only authority, to restrain a man from working at a lawful trade. But on the other hand, "Common law did ever allow free trade." [67] It is for this reason, among others, that the courts were apt to interpret leniently acts of Parliament which tended to restrain trade and interfere with property.

We can see the problems growing out of Parliament's inva-

[65] *Ibid.*, p. 200.

[66] Gardiner, *History of England*, I, 356.

[67] *Commons Debates*, 1621, ed. Notestein, Relf, Simpson, II, 181. This was put forward against the monopoly of issuing licenses for innkeepers.

sions of property rights reflected in the cases dealing with the Statute of Uses. The idea that land or chattel could be held by one person to the use of another dates back to the early middle ages. The Crusades, for example, drew a large number of land-owners away from their homes, and we find frequent examples of crusaders conveying their lands to friends at home upon various conditions, which were usually cast in the form of a use. For those who had the use of land or chattel there were advantages under the complications of the common law of real property. They could dispose of the land by will, and settlements could be drawn with much greater freedom than under the common law. The use thus developed into a more convenient way of holding land, yet the use was open to many abuses. It could be used to defraud creditors, for the land of the debtor could be transformed into a use, and he who now had the use of the land could not be made to pay the debt of the owner. Moreover, the use could not be brought into harmony with the feudal system. It became a means of circumventing the duties owed to the lord through conveying the land as use and thus defrauding the lord of such of his revenues as wardship, marriage, and relief. As the most important lord of the realm, the monarchy was the financial loser through this circumventing of feudal dues by means of uses.

This consideration prompted Henry VIII to sponsor the Statute of Uses (1536). Under the Statute, he who had the "use" of the land became invested with the benefits and responsibilities of the legal owner. Thus the lord's revenues were assured, and uses could no longer be used to circumvent the common law.[68] The Statute of Uses amounted to a transfer of property rights from the owner to him who had the "use" of the land. Here the King in Parliament invaded the rights of property, asserting its sovereign authority in a manner not justifiable under the law of nature. How could this fact be inte-

[68] The summary is largely taken from Theodore F. Plucknett, *A Concise History of the Common Law* (Rochester: Lawyers' Cooperative Publishing Co., 1929), p. 371 ff.

grated with the property-protecting nature of the common law as a reflection of the law of nature?

In 1606, for example, the judges declared certain vague provisions in the Statute unlawful, for "God forbid that the inheritances and estates of men should depend on such uncertainty." [69] Bacon had piously asserted that the Statute of Uses "would not stir or turmoil possessions settled at common law." [70] However optimistic Bacon might have been in this regard, in the end the overriding authority of a statute had to be accepted. Of the conflict between common law and Parliament, we shall say more later, but it demonstrates well the complete powers of Parliament over property by the end of Elizabeth's reign, about which all that Coke could say here was

. . . acts of Parliament that are made against the freedom of trade, merchandising, handicrafts and mysteries, never live long.[71]

But such acts had to be obeyed while in force, for Parliament was the "highest and most honorable and absolute court of justice in England." [72]

Coke's reluctant assertion that even acts of Parliament in restraint of trade had to be respected is perhaps the best illustration of the complete acceptance, for better or for worse, of Parliament as the custodian of every Englishman's property. Yet this acceptance of Parliament's power over property on the part of the lawyers and courts was a relatively new development by the time Coke wrote. By the middle of the sixteenth century the judges as yet had their doubts whether an act of Parliament could change property by its mere fiat.[73] When the adjustment to the actual facts took place, the result of the

[69] Sir Edward Coke, *Reports etc.* (Edinburgh, 1907), LXXVII, 316, Sir Anthony Mildmay's Case.

[70] Sir Francis Bacon, "Reading on the Statute of Uses," *Works of Sir Francis Bacon*, ed. Spedding and Heath (London, 1892), VII, 425.

[71] Sir Edward Coke, *Fourth Institutes* (London, 1797), p. 31.

[72] Sir Edward Coke, *First Institutes* (London, 1794), chap. x, sect. 164, lib. II.

[73] Edward T. Lampson, "Some New Light on the Growth of Parliamentary Sovereignty, Wimbish versus Taillebois," *American Political Science Review*, XXV (October, 1941), 952-960.

weakening concept of natural law becomes apparent. Even before Smith wrote his treatise, typical of the new trends, devoid
of supernatural law, the judges seem to have gone far toward
the recognition of Parliament's powers. By 1559 the learned
judges were able to state, "An act of Parliament or the common
law, may make an estate void as to one and good as to another,
but a man by his words and the breath of his mouth cannot do
it." [74] Where were the concepts of natural law which forbade
such interference?

In 1606 the judges again stated that "an Act of Parliament
may make an estate cease as if one were dead." [75] In the arguments of Chudleigh's case (1589–95), dealing with the Statute
of Uses, we have a striking example of the reluctant adjustments
to the actual fact of Parliament's power over sovereignty. In this
case the judges were arguing the matter of estates growing out
of the Statute. So important was this argument considered that
the final judgments took place in the exchequer chamber before
all of the justices. [76] The Statute of Uses, the judges held, was
passed only in order to make a plain and full restitution of the
common law: [77] there were two inventors of uses—fear and
fraud, "fear in times of troubles and civil wars . . . and frauds
to defeat due debts, lawful actions." [78] What is more, he who
had the use of the estate had no remedy but in Chancery, and
the Chancellor had no right to determine inheritances. [79] Uses,
then, were not like commons, rents, and conditions, which were
ordinary hereditaments in judgment of law, and which could
not be taken away and discontinued. [80] Thus the makers of the
Statute had come to the conclusion that uses were so subtle that
they could not merely be reformed; "and therefore, as a skillful
gardener will not cut away the leaves of the weeds, but extirpate

[74] Coke, *Reports etc.*, LXXXVI, 197, Corbet's Case.
[75] *Ibid.*, LXXVII, 313, Sir Anthony Mildmay's Case.
[76] *Ibid.*, LXXVI, 273.
[77] *Ibid.*, p. 282.
[78] *Ibid.*, p. 275.
[79] *Ibid.*, p. 278.
[80] *Ibid.*, pp. 277-279.

them by the roots"—they extirpated them.[81] The common law, therefore, and in the opinion of the judges, would not uphold "these subtle and fraudulent uses," because as appears by judgment of all the Parliament, they were subversive to the common law.[82]

Here the judges rationalized this transfer of property by Parliament. The key to their argument seems to be the intent of the Statute to weed out this practice as subversive to the common law. The judges were arguing from the preamble of the Statute. Bacon pleaded in this case:

Our preambles are annexed for exposition, and this gives aim to the body of the statute, for the preamble sets up the mark and the body of the law levels at it.[83]

It is therefore highly fallacious to compare the preamble of a statute to the leading article in a daily paper. Do our lawyers plead leading articles as determining the intent of a law, and do our judges accept them as such? [84] Here the preamble giving the purpose of the Statute facilitated the transition on the part of the judges to an acceptance of Parliament's power over property. And as Parliament had judged uses to be subversive to the common law, the judges were bound to agree.

Is this not reminiscent of the saying of Christopher St. Germain that Parliament will not recite anything against the truth? Indeed, we now find the judges toward the turn of the century implying that acts of Parliament are the custodians of religion, justice, and truth.

All Statutes which are made to suppress wrong, or to take away fraud, or to prevent the decay of religion, justice, and truth, shall

[81] *Ibid.*, p. 283.

[82] *Ibid.*, p. 298.

[83] Quoted in *A Discourse upon the Statutes etc.*, ed. Samuel E. Thorne (San Marino: Henry E. Huntington Library, 1942), p. 114 (n. 28).

[84] W. S. Holdsworth, *History of English Law* (Boston: Little, Brown, 1927), IV, 460. "The sixteenth century equivalent of a leading article in a government newspaper upon a government measure." Dr. T. F. Plucknett quotes Holdsworth's assertion without contradiction in Plucknett, *A Concise History of the Common Law*, p. 380.

bind the king. . . . For religion, justice, and truth are the sure supporters of the crowns and diadems of kings.[85]

The idea of St. Germain that Parliament would not recite anything against the truth seems to have become an accepted judicial fact and indeed Coke was to repeat it verbatim in his *Institutes*.[86] The case of Chudleigh seems to indicate the way in which the transition to the acceptance by the courts of full parliamentary power over property was accomplished.

There was still an attempt to preserve the traditional concept against the Statute. This hesitancy was well illustrated when Justice Gaudy stated that ". . . the statute of 27 H. 8 did not extend to subvert and destroy uses in other manners, than by the executing and transferring of the possession of the land to them." [87] The judges then went on to limit the statute to uses in *esse*, or in consideration of the law. They exempted uses in contingency or in future.[88] But for all that, the judges recognized the basic transfer of land which was entailed by the statute even if they did so on the pretense of a restoration of ancient law.[89] By the end of the century the idea that Parliament could make an estate void as to one man and good as to another had taken firm root. The judgment of Parliament had to be adhered to. Arguments of natural law were not openly discussed in these decisions. However, what Sir Thomas Smith was asserting in his *Republica*, that Parliament could change the possessions of private men, was becoming accepted in the courts of law.

Once the King in Parliament was recognized as possessing jurisdiction over property, this right had, of course, to be denied to the king out of Parliament, even if the king, like James, hinted at this right in the name of his office as the father of his

[85] Coke, *Reports etc.*, LXXVII, 70, Case of Ecclesiastical Persons.
[86] Coke, *Fourth Institutes*, p. 342.
[87] Coke, *Reports etc.*, LXXVI, 305.
[88] *Ibid.*, p. 308.
[89] *Ibid.*, p. 303, ". . . and as the use shall be so shall be the possession by force of the Statute . . . the possession shall be transferred to it by force of the statute."

people. There was little talk of a natural law which protected property from both king and Parliament.

Parliament's consciousness of its custodianship of property rights is well illustrated by its proceedings against the merchant adventurers. The Commons feared that this powerful group was escaping from its grasp. As Sandys put it, "In Genua a Company of St. George, now grown so great as independent of the State." [90] When a member of Parliament exclaimed, "He that hath no propriety in his goods, is not free," he did not mean that Parliament when necessary could not dispose of the goods of free men.[91]

There was still a certain sphere in which the king's right to property not strictly his own was recognized. Justice Coke stated that all property must be in some person. But such goods as no subject could claim as his own belong to the king by his prerogative. This category covered such items as treasure troves, strays, and wrecks of the sea.[92] Sir Francis Bacon made a similar statement. But typically enough, he applied it to the property which is in persons and not just to the residue of un-claimed possessions. "No man is so absolute owner of his posses-sions, but that the wisdom of the law does reserve certain titles unto others," and these others were the king, the lords, and the tenants. The law favored the king wherever he shared in the possessions, for "No law doth endow the king or sovereign with more prerogatives or privileges than ours." [93] Bacon's view seemed to give the king a dangerous wedge into the prop-erty rights of his subjects. As we shall see, Coke's view was more typical of parliamentary opinion than was Bacon's.

In spite of this limited sphere in which the king could be allowed jurisdiction over property, the King in Parliament de-termined possessions as far as both Parliament itself and the courts were concerned. Stimulated by rising economic pros-

---

[90] *Journal of the House of Commons*, 5 May, 1623, p. 699.

[91] *Ibid.*, 9 April, 1624, p. 759.

[92] Coke, *Second Institutes*, pt. I, 167.

[93] Bacon, "Reading on the Statute of Uses," *Works*, ed. Spedding and Heath (1892), VII, 420, 421.

perity, Parliament's claim over property cut through all bonds of natural law. Jean Bodin would hardly have seen in such pretensions a *droit gouvernement*.

Whitelocke was thus voicing a sentiment in tune with the times when he stated that only the King in Parliament could change property. But Parliament was soon to go even beyond Whitelocke himself in its claims to sovereignty. It will be well to treat of Parliament's quests in this direction as implied in the matter of foreign policy and in the events leading to the Petition of Right before coming back to its function as sole lawmaking body and sole judge in relation to the king's courts. It is in its property claims and in its grasping for executive powers that we reach the furthest extent of its claims. It is in the quest for executive power that we can also observe, in some detail, the fatal mingling of economic and religious issues which, together with the blunders of the king, served to spur on Parliament's quest for sovereignty practically in spite of itself.

VI

†

THE MAKING OF WAR AND PEACE had been to Jean Bodin one of the inalienable marks of sovereign power. This mark of sovereign power in England had been reserved to the king, even by writers like Sir Thomas Smith, who conceded other vast powers to the King in Parliament. Nothing illustrates better the growing pretensions of Parliament than its claim to control over this vital part of the royal prerogative, and this not so much because the assertion of these powers was made in a conscious way by Parliament as because matters of foreign policy became bound up with religious and economic issues. Here once again it was the actual course of events which led to Parliament's claims and there was on this point relatively little theorizing.

When Whitelocke gave us his argument concerning the sovereign power of Parliament, he did not include foreign affairs, nor does the Petition of 1610 make any claims in that direction. But eleven years later, the Petition of 1621 crowned Parliament's claims by flatly asserting that no matters regarding the government or the benefit of the realm were without its purview. "What greater prerogative is there than to make war, matches and alliances?" [1]

The first seeds of parliamentary discontent with James's foreign policy had already been sown by the time Whitelocke spoke. In 1604 James made peace with Spain. It was not a satisfactory peace from the commercial point of view. English merchants had not been given the right to trade in Spanish possessions.[2] Moreover, it seemed that the Protestant Netherlands had been abandoned to Spain and that Elizabeth's traditional policy of aid to the besieged provinces had been successfully reversed. The Venetian ambassador reported that James spoke of the Netherlands as rebels and that such bad example, in his opinion, should not be encouraged.[3] Thus the king's political philosophy in this instance, at any rate, helped to further incline him toward the cause of Spain. The underlying precept of James's foreign policy was to bring about a peaceful settlement of the religious problems which were dividing Europe. Spain and England, the chief Catholic and the chief Protestant powers, if allied, might bring peace to Europe.[4] This peace policy seems not unconnected with James's attempt to divide active from passive Catholics in England, and to extend toleration to those who believed merely in the "spiritual" headship of the Pope.[5] To this policy James conformed even when it became obvious that any real Catholic had to believe in the visible as well as in the invisible power of the papacy.[6] James's

[1] *Commons Debates,* 1621, ed. Notestein, Relf, Simpson (New Haven: Yale University Press, 1935), II, 488.

[2] G. Davies, *The Early Stuarts* (Oxford: The Clarendon Press, 1937), p. 45.

[3] Giovanni Cerlo Scaramelli to the Doge and Senate, May 28, 1603. *Calendar of State Papers,* Venetian (1603-1607), X, No. 66, p. 40.

[4] S. R. Gardiner in *The Cambridge Modern History* (New York: Macmillan, 1905), III, 558. On James's views on peace see *The Peace-maker or Great Britain's Blessing* (London, 1618), probably written by James himself. Dedicated to "all our loving and peace embracing subjects." On the other hand it has been asserted that four thousand pounds difference in the dowries of the French princess and the infanta decided James in favor of the latter.

[5] W. H. Frere, *A History of the English Church in the Reigns of Elizabeth and James I* (London: Macmillan, 1904), p. 336.

[6] W. K. Jordan, *The Development of Toleration in England from the Accession of James I to the Convention of the Long Parliament* (Cambridge,

stubborn attempt to hold to a line of action once he had begun it was as obvious in his foreign policy as in his domestic policies.

Thus James's plan for the marriage of his son to the infanta of Spain, which would seal an alliance, was pushed relentlessly. In 1611 Salisbury, sensing public opinion in a way in which his master never did, was able to prevent the match from succeeding.[7] With Salisbury's death James fell more and more under the tutelage of the Spanish faction at court, which was led by the secretly Catholic Northampton.[8] James, however, refused to comply with Spain's demand that he ask Parliament to repeal the penal laws against the Catholics (even he must have known that this was a hopeless request), and negotiations were again broken off.[9] Yet James persisted, and in 1621 he took up the negotiations once again, in spite of the fact that such an action was bound to produce serious repercussions in Parliament,[10] for by that time the Thirty Years' War had broken out in Europe and James's son-in-law, Frederick, was forced to flee the Palatinate before the advance of the Catholic forces led by the Emperor Ferdinand II.

Frederick was a Protestant and a Calvinist to boot. His marriage to James's daughter in 1612 had been popular in England, where Parliament was perhaps by that time already predominantly Puritan.[11] Here indeed was a rallying point for the anti-Spanish faction led by the Puritans. There was a martial enthusiasm in Parliament with little or no thought of English isolation from the European struggle.[12] It was to prove fatal

---

Mass.: Harvard University Press, 1936), p. 79. Especially inasmuch as the Pope was determining his English policy according to the wishes of the Jesuits.

[7] Gardiner in *The Cambridge Modern History*, III, 559.

[8] *Ibid.*, p. 560.

[9] *Ibid.*, p. 561.

[10] S. R. Gardiner, *History of England, 1603–1642* (London: Longmans, Green & Co., 1883), II, 28. James even expressed to Gondomar the hope that a reconciliation with Rome might be possible on a purely spiritual basis, and this only three days after the meeting of the Parliament of 1621.

[11] Frere, *A History of the English Church*, p. 378.

[12] *The Court and Times of James I*, ed. Thomas Birch (London, 1849), p. 378.

that, in view of this enthusiasm, James persisted in his foreign policy. The sentiment of a subaltern court could not, however, affect his Scottish stubbornness. After all, foreign policy was his lawful prerogative. James never seemed to realize the strength and determination of the interests which united Parliament behind Frederick and against Spain. The religious ire of the Puritans was aroused. As Pym put it, popery in reality sought absolute control over all things, and therefore Protestant and Catholic could never be friends.[13]

And the phrase "over all things" was not devoid of conscious economic connotations. English merchants were forbidden to trade in Spanish possessions. They were attacked by the Inquisition in Spain herself. Even before issues of foreign policy became paramount, Parliament had been greatly concerned with the question of whether James's treaty with Spain included the importation into England of Spanish tobacco, something which Parliament wanted to forbid.[14] Perhaps the best and clearest statement of Parliament's war aims against Spain was given by Sir John Eliot in 1623: "Our common interests all at hazard, our friends at pawn, religion at stake. . . . Are we poor? Spain [is] rich: that our Indies. Breaking with them, we shall break our necessities together." [15] The religious and economic interests of the members of Parliament were intertwined and thus involved in the struggle taking place on the other side of the Rhine.

There is ample record of the state of popular opinion outside the houses of Parliament. Spaniards were attacked in the Exchange by anonymous gentlemen. The Spanish ambassador and his retinue were publicly insulted by the excitable apprentices of London. When the apprentices were consequently led off to punishment, they were rescued by three hundred people "of all sorts." Gondomar fled to the king's palace at None-

[13] *Commons Debates*, 1621, ed. Notestein, Relf, Simpson, II, 461-464.
[14] *Ibid.*, II, 213-214.
[15] *Journal of the House of Commons*, 19 March, 1623, p. 740.

such.[16] Anti-Spanish propagandists like Thomas Scott, typically enough a divine, had a field day. Even the shadow of the Earl of Essex was resurrected to spite Spain.[17] And Parliament in the meantime was protesting the mistreatment of English merchants on Spanish soil.

To continue a policy of reconciliation with Spain at this point was bound to produce a clash with Parliament. Perhaps there were some in Parliament who knew, as James did not seem to know, that Spanish aid was largely responsible for the Catholic emperor's successes in Germany.[18] It is clear that foreign policy affected the interests of Parliament too vitally to remain for long an undisputed *arcana imperii.*

In February, 1621, the Commons had still been satisfied with Privy Councilor Calvert's assertion that the king need not consult the subjects about the waging of war.[19] James had even been voted a substantial subsidy.[20] Parliament sat back and waited, attacking meanwhile both Spanish commercial practices and those at home who opposed Frederick's cause.[21] As time wore on there was some plainer speaking, but, as yet, no open discussion of foreign policies. The Bohemian issue was mentioned only in connection with the decay of trade at home and so linked up with the generally decayed state of England.[22] It is a curious and ironic fact that it was actually the govern-

[16] *The Court and Times of James I,* Meddus to Meade, April 6, 1621, II, 246; *ibid.,* Meade to Stutteville, April 9, 1621, *ibid.,* p. 247; Chamberlain to Carlton, February 10, 1621, *ibid.,* p. 222.

[17] See Thomas R. Scott, *News from Parnassus* (Utrecht, 1622), *Vox Regis* (1623), or his *Robert Earle of Essex his Ghost* (1624). There is also the anonymous *An Apology of the Earle of Essex penned by Himself 1598* (1603), which appeared just before James made peace with Spain. See also Louis B. Wright, "Propaganda against James I. 'Appeasement' of Spain," *Huntington Library Quarterly,* VI (February, 1943), 149-172.

[18] C. V. Wedgwood, *The Thirty Years War* (New Haven: Yale University Press, 1939); chap. i, chap. x.

[19] *Commons Debates,* 1621, ed. Notestein, Relf, Simpson, II, 88, 89.

[20] *Ibid.,* II, 92.

[21] *Ibid.,* II, 294; IV, 232-233.

[22] *Ibid.,* III, 344-346.

ment which provided the impetus for the Commons' debate on foreign policy, and thereby endangered one of the king's most cherished prerogatives.

At the beginning of the new session, in November, 1621, Lord Digby submitted to the Commons a thorough outline of the policies of the king's government. In itself this was nothing new. Ever since the last decade of Queen Elizabeth's reign, the Privy Council had been careful, as a courtesy to the House, to explain policies and to outline the reasons for them.[23] But Lord Digby went one step further. He actually discussed James's foreign policies and told the House that his master's peaceful policies had failed and that war was now the last resort.[24] Only one year previously James had issued another stringent proclamation against open discussion of matters of state and especially of foreign affairs, which seemed to have been discussed frequently and in public.[25] Was Lord Digby here exceeding his authority? Or was his admission, followed as it was by the treasurer's statement, meant to call forth a speedier subsidy? Sir Edward Coke realized the novelty of the procedure and its inevitable consequences when he accused Digby and the Lords of initiating the whole debate on foreign policy.[26] Coke was to write in his *Institutes*, "To the King only belongs the authority to levy war. In subjects it is high treason." [27] But about the levying of war abroad, Parliament now wanted to have its way. It was useless for Weston, the Chancellor of the Exchequer, to explain, "It is good when the king advises with his Parliament of war but for the Parliament to advise the king of war is presumptuous." [28] The floodgates had opened:

---

[23] W. Notestein, *The Winning of the Initiative of the House of Commons* (London: Oxford University, 1924), p. 137.

[24] *Commons Debates*, 1621, ed. Notestein, Relf, Simpson, III, 422.

[25] *Royal Proclamation*, 24 December, 1620.

[26] *Commons Debates*, 1621, ed. Notestein, Relf, Simpson, II, 502.

[27] Sir Edward Coke, *Third Institutes* (London, 1797), p. 9.

[28] *Commons Debates*, 1621, ed. Notestein, Relf, Simpson, II, 489. Wentworth answered typically enough that it concerns the natural body to provide for the safety of its head: "The King is never greater than in Parliament and we can never approach more nearly to our head than there," p. 490.

the prerogative of peace and war lay open to the public gaze.

That the attacks against Spain by the Commons seemed to have been justified was made even clearer when Digby underlined that while England's way had been peace, Spain's way was war.[29] The harvest was speedily reaped. Three days after Digby's statement Alford rose in the Commons. With bitter sarcasm he railed against the impotency of the House to discuss affairs of religion in Bohemia, these being "matters of state" and forbidden by proclamation. Secretary Calvert was forced to state promptly that such a proclamation had meant to cover only discussions in ale houses and like places.[30] By this reply, intended no doubt to mollify the temper of the House and to encourage a subsidy, the door was left wide open for a debate on foreign policy. This was a very shortsighted step, for it had necessarily to lead in the end to the claim that Parliament was a fit place to discuss matters of state. "The king," said one member of Parliament, "has his council, but in *arduis rebus* this council of state in these urgent businesses." [31] Here Parliament was elaborating its doctrine of *raison d'état*. And for Parliament this seemed to have meant that in such *arduis rebus* it had to be consulted.

The idea of Parliament as a council of state was not new, for we find it voiced, for example, in 1605 by Whitelocke. But then it was concerned with legal privileges.[32] By 1621 this doctrine seems to have been consciously applied in order to usurp matters which had been clearly within the king's sphere of government.

The debate on foreign policy followed promptly. It was to bring to light again the real motives for the Commons' eager support of Frederick and hatred of Spain. Crewe, for example, began his discourse by speaking of the riches of the Indies, only to advocate the suppression of the papists.[33] Members of Parliament began to come down to the practical details of the waging

[29] *Ibid.*, III, 446.
[30] *Ibid.*, II, 441.
[31] *Ibid.*, II, 505.
[32] *Vide supra*, p. 87.
[33] *Commons Debates, 1621*, ed. Notestein, Relf, Simpson, II, 451.

of the war. Digges suggested an attack on the Spanish fleet as a means of bankrupting that kingdom.[34]

All of this was about a nation with which James was still at peace. Of what use were the Lord Treasurer's warnings that policy was the king's preserve, when a Mr. Neal arose and prayed, "God direct our war"?[35] It was, typically enough, in the Committee on Religion that Pym made his great speech posing the true dilemma of Parliament. While denouncing Spain with vigor, Pym dwelled long on James's qualities of friendship, bounty, and wisdom, which had been utterly abused.[36] Parliament might debate foreign policy, but the king, for all his weaknesses, was still the executive.

Meanwhile, the House had been drawing up a document to be presented to James. From our point of view the most important clause within this Petition of 1621 was the wish that James would publicly support the Protestant princes. Here indeed Parliament was taking a second step, from mere debate to actual advice to the king on a matter of peace and war.

Did the House realize the importance of the step it was taking? At least Sir Edward Coke realized the gravity of the situation. He frankly recognized the illegality of such advice on the part of Parliament, but on the other hand he took refuge in the fact that this was to be merely a "petition of grace" and not of right.[37] Indeed, Coke with his strong sense of historical precedent even went so far as to suggest that the House might not be solely competent to decide cases of freedom of speech when they arose out of matters pertaining to foreign affairs.[38] On the other hand, nothing could show better the eventual and inevitable acceptance of Parliament's claims than that Coke took up a different position when it came to writing the *Fourth Institutes*. There he included both the state of the kingdom and

[34] *Ibid.*, II, 445-452.
[35] *Ibid.*, II, 452.
[36] *Ibid.*, II, 461-464.
[37] *Ibid.*, II, 495-496.
[38] *Ibid.*, II, 57 (n. 11).

its defense, as well as the state of the church and its defense, under matters to be handled in Parliament.[39]

Others, too, counseled caution at the time.[40] But the only result of this hesitancy was the insertion in the petition of a clause disclaiming any intention of touching the prerogative. James thought differently. He decided to act before the petition was presented. In a message to the House he told its members not to debate matters "far above their reach and capacity." [41] James did not stop here. He went on to question the very essence of the privileges of Parliament, asserting his power to punish any man's misdemeanor in Parliament or out of it.

Not all the stormy sessions of Parliament could make James change his theories of prerogative. He was in the right: even Coke by implication had admitted this. But this outspoken message produced consternation in the House. It had to be read three times. Hakewill plucked up the spirit of the House by reading some lines from the Apology of 1604.[42] The House continued doggedly to frame its petition. James might tear it from the journals and dissolve his Parliament, but it still marked the assumption by Parliament of what had undoubtedly been royal prerogatives. The idea that all governmental matters, as well as ecclesiastical, came within the compass of Parliament was a revolutionary one. Parliament here laid a claim to control over a vital mark of sovereignty. It was to be more than just a claim. The fates seemed to unite against James's policies. Charles and Buckingham returned disgruntled and empty handed from their last expedition to Madrid, disappointed wooers for the hand of the infanta. They now became powerful allies of the war party, and the main strength of the war party lay in Parliament. The failure of James's peace policy and the imminence of war made subsidies more important than ever and had at least one very important consequence.

[39] Sir Edward Coke, *Fourth Institutes* (London, 1797), p. 9.

[40] *Commons Debates*, 1621, ed. Notestein, Relf, Simpson, II, 441, 487 (n. 6).

[41] *Ibid.*, II, 500. Message in Sir G. Prothero, *Statutes etc.* (Oxford: Oxford University Press, 1913), p. 310.

[42] *Commons Debates*, 1621, ed. Notestein, Relf, Simpson, II, 501-502. "Let us petition and petition again . . . till he hears us." (Mr. Delbridge), p. 500 .

In Lord Digby's frank address on foreign affairs at the opening of the Parliament in 1623, James not only asked the Commons' advice on his relation with Spain, but also on the proposed match of the prince.[43] It is as if he had recognized the Petition of 1621 and had followed its principles. Ten days later the Chancellor of the Exchequer told the house that "His Majesty now desires our opinion whether he shall trust to these suppositions [made to him by Spain] or trust to his own legs." [44] Here indeed Parliament was receiving good training in the management of foreign policy. Moreover, in his opening speech before Parliament a year later, in 1624, James actually felt himself forced to justify the failure of his policies. What was worse, he actually asked the advice of the Commons on these former *arcana imperii*. Was it with irony that James exclaimed, "never king gave more trust to his subjects"? [45]

James had been converted to a war policy. Harmony, he might have thought, would now be restored. But once again James misjudged, failing completely to understand the deeper aims of the men in Parliament. James wanted to fight the war in order to recapture the Palatinate for Frederick. But the Palatinate had been of little interest to Parliament. It had merely served as a rallying point against the real enemy, Spain. It was a direct attack on Spain which Parliament favored, and here again, largely for commercial and religious reasons.[46] The decision on a war policy, therefore, did not bring about any great unanimity of views between James and his trusted subjects. But this time the issue was to be decided between them. Buckingham, constantly rising in favor and influence with James, sided with Parliament. However, he counseled piratical expeditions rather than open war.[47] It was Buckingham who persuaded James to take the initiative in another fateful step toward transforming Parliament's claims into a reality.

[43] *Journal of the House of Commons*, I, 19 February, 1623, p. 670.

[44] *Journal of the House of Commons*, I, 27 February, 1623, p. 721.

[45] S. R. Gardiner, *History of England under Buckingham and Charles I* (London: Longmans, Green & Co., 1875), I, 13.

[46] *Ibid.*, I, 28.

[47] *Ibid.*, I, 21-22.

James authorized the House to appoint a committee to "see the issuing out of money they give for the recovery of the Palatinate." [48] Here indeed the House was given a measure of actual control over the prosecution of the war. Apparently it had taken only a small step from criticism of foreign policy to financial control over it. James tried, to be sure, to minimize this concession granted under Buckingham's influence. The war, he stated (after the Commons had joyfully voted a subsidy), was now a matter for military men, not to be ordered by a multitude.[49] Yet the precedent had been set. In the end James broke off the treaty with Spain.[50] Parliament's aims and policies seemed to have triumphed all along the line.

In a large measure the eventual triumph of Parliament's policies was due to Buckingham. He had used Parliament to further his policies, which happened to be identical with those of the Commons. His sway over James explains concessions which were in such great conflict with James's idea of his prerogatives. James had not changed. In his last speech to the Parliament before his death, he once again decided to use the idea of reason of state in order to tamper with the preface to the subsidy bill of the House. And he told the Commons as much. He rightly warned Buckingham against creating dangerous parliamentary precedents just for the success of the moment.[51] But it was well for the growing power of Parliament that Buckingham was essentially an opportunist.

Parliament's actual control over finance with regard to peace and war was not to be of lasting importance. But a precedent had been set. Peace and war had been debated in Parliament, Parliament's advice had been sought in these matters by the king, and its policies had triumphed. Parliament had laid a strong claim to control over the power of war and peace as marks of sovereignty.

[48] *Ibid.*, I, 25.
[49] *Ibid.*, I, 33.
[50] *Ibid.*, I, 45.
[51] *Ibid.*, I, 65.

Was there any theoretical justification for such claims? We have seen that Coke realized the novelty of the step which was being taken. We have also seen how the government itself brought on the discussion. There was, therefore, little need for theorizing. It was clear that to a large extent the desire for subsidy had led the government to undertake these steps.

> The Lords and Commons cannot be charged with anything for the defense of the realm . . . unless it be by their will in Parliament. That is, in the grant of a subsidy, whereunto the king assented.[52]

Once again the power of the purse led to the enhancement of Parliament's powers.

It does not seem to have occurred to James that, with Smith and Fortescue as his authorities, he could have levied taxes in an emergency without Parliament's consent, once war had been decided on.[53] Such theoretical justification as there was on the part of Parliament seems to have turned around the idea that Parliament must concern itself with the common good of the realm.

> Let us look into the estate and government, and, finding that which is amiss, make this Parliament the reformer of the commonwealth. . . .[54]

Indeed, it was on such grounds that Alford opposed the king's proclamation against meddling in matters of state. Speaking in the House he stated,

> . . . that we should not meddle with the business of the Palatinate . . . is the precedent wherein we are warily to proceed, for hereafter the king may else say, we shall meddle only with this or that business . . . for hereafter if we shall touch on anything for the

---

[52] Sir Edward Coke, *Second Institutes* (London, 1797), pt. I, 61.

[53] *Vide supra*, chap. i.

[54] *Parliamentary Debates*, 1625, ed. S. R. Gardiner (Camden Society, 1873), p. 82.

good of the commonwealth his majesty may be incensed and so dissolve Parliament.[55]

Moreover, the idea of the common good must always be exempted from such treaties as the king makes. Even if a treaty, such as the treaty with Spain, be made, it must have a saving clause, excepting the laws of the kingdom, both those in force and the power of making laws for the good of the state.[56] The idea of the common good seems also to have been fundamental in Parliament's idea of the "reason of state" as residing within the walls of Parliament. It need hardly be pointed out that, in fighting for jurisdiction over foreign policy, Parliament also fought against James's views of the reason of state, which forbade them to meddle with the main points of government: "that is my craft." [57]

This concept of the common good as being in Parliament's custody could also be applied to bolster claims to control over such unpopular royal practices as monopolies. Monopolies were generally evil because the common good was to be preferred before the good of single persons or even of particular towns of the kingdom.[58] It is obvious that Parliament regarded itself as qualified to judge of the common good. Parliament might even confirm a monopoly if it was judged to be for the good of the state.[59] For James, on the other hand, as we have seen, the good of the state resided in the king, who in *arduis rebus* could override all constitutional limitations.[60]

Thus Parliament here elaborated its own concept of reason of state, and applied it to foreign policy as well as to commercial matters. When Alford exclaimed in the Parliament of 1621: ". . . but if patents and monopolies and the like be ac-

[55] *Commons Debates and Proceedings*, 1620 and 1621, ed. E. Nicholas (Oxford, 1766), II, 197.

[56] *Commons Debates*, 1621, ed. Notestein, Relf, Simpson, IV, 227.

[57] James I, "Speech of 1609," p. 315.

[58] *Commons Debates*, 1621, ed. Notestein, Relf, Simpson, IV, 252.

[59] *Ibid.*, II, 350.

[60] *Vide supra*, chap. iv.

counted matters of state, *pereat res publica,*" it was of the king's concept of *raison d'état* that he was thinking.[61] But by 1621, Parliament itself had elaborated a rival concept. By that date even Sir Edward Coke could state that Parliament ". . . may treat anything concerning the king, state and church. . . ." [62] On other occasions he was forced to intimate that Parliament might not be competent to decide matters pertaining to foreign affairs.[63] But here were the crossroads, for from now on men were increasingly forced to choose between the king and his Parliaments. Coke's hesitating admission of Parliament's omnicompetence in administrative matters demonstrates the road along which he was to travel in the 1620's, while men like Wentworth and Hyde in turn were to abandon the cause of a "revolutionary" Parliament for the cause of the king.

The question of reason of state was, however, to have another effect on the dispute between king and Parliament. Its impact on the growth of parliamentary sovereignty, apart from the matter of foreign affairs, can be seen in the question of arbitrary imprisonment for forced loans, which came to a head in 1628. Here, in a manner, the whole dispute as to where reason of state resided came into sharp focus. Obviously, if the king could imprison a man merely for reason of state, without stating the cause of imprisonment, arbitrary rule was a distinct possibility. Of what avail was it that Englishmen were freemen, if the king could take away this freedom as he listed? The struggle against the king on this count was a practical one, waged by Parliament for concrete ends, just as the dispute over foreign policy had been for Parliament a concrete fight with a definite end in view. As Selden said at the first conference of the Houses of Parliament on this problem, a right is useless without a remedy. If there was no remedy provided by inferior courts, Parliament must provide one.[64]

[61] *Commons Debates and Proceedings,* 1620 and 1621, ed. E. Nicholas, II, 109.

[62] *Commons Debates,* 1621, ed. Notestein, Relf, Simpson, II, 541-542.

[63] *Ibid.,* II, 57 (n. 11).

[64] *Journal of the House of Lords,* III, 9 April, 1628, pp. 722, 731.

Moreover, inasmuch as the idea of matter of state was being used to extort forced loans by arbitrary imprisonment, the whole matter of the property rights of the subject were involved in the dispute. "It is an undoubted and fundamental point," exclaimed Sir Dudley Digges, "of this so ancient a law of England, that the subjects have a true property in their good, lands, and possessions," and this was "lately prejudiced by some pressures . . . because they have been pursued by imprisonment contrary to the law," the more as legal redress had failed.[65]

So far no one could object to the arguments. Fortescue himself had subscribed to the medieval maxim: to the king, authority over all, to private persons, property. But as the debate wore on it became obvious that the whole idea of reason of state as residing in the king was being attacked, as well as that Parliament wanted a definite control over the executive power of the monarch. These points are best brought out in connection with the remarkable argument of Sergeant Ashley before the joint committees of Parliament. Against the Commons' assertions that imprisonment without cause shown was against the common law, Ashley put forward the assertion that the common law was by no means the only law of England. There was the ecclesiastical law, the admiralty law, and the law of state. The law of state can proceed according to natural equity, "and infinite are the occurrents of state unto which the common law extends not. . . ." The king's power is from God. "Shall we conceive that our king has so far transmitted the power of his sword to inferior magistrates that he hath not reserved so much supreme power as to commit an offender to prison?"[66] Evidently both Houses did so conceive, for the Lords censured Ashley for his speech and he had to make an humble submission.[67] That in itself was a startling repudiation of Ashley's ideas. Indeed, the Commons went so far as to refuse to include a clause sponsored by the Lords saving the king's sovereign power in the petition which they were now, in 1628, prepar-

[65] *Ibid.*, III, 9 April, 1628, p. 718.
[66] *Ibid.*, 19 April, 1628, pp. 758-759.
[67] *Ibid.*

ing. The words "sovereign power" as applied to the king, they held, were not fit words for the petition.[68] They were opposed to the whole amendment which the Lords proposed:

... due regard to leave entire that sovereign power wherewith your Majesty is trusted, for the protection, safety and happiness of your people.[69]

They wanted to control this power, not to leave it intact.

Yet the protection of the people had been one of the cardinal attributes of the monarch for both Fortescue and the Tudor writers. But we must remember that the Commons' interference with foreign affairs had already sapped the power of that concept. Their petition was to be one of "right" and not of "grace." [70] It was not fit that a saving clause be added to it, "That these words [of Sovereign power] were not words used to be inserted in the law, nor legal"; they did not however propose to meddle with the king's sovereignty.[71] Indeed, they constantly stressed that, just like Magna Carta, the petition they were preparing was merely affirmative of the law.[72] This may have been the case,[73] though Dr. Relf questions the accuracy of their precedents. But fundamentally the whole issue of reason of state was at stake and with it the king's executive powers. The Houses' reaction to Ashley's speech showed this clearly. Distrust of the king went hand in hand with the attempt to curb his powers.

Again, the Houses' reaction to the king's attorney's speech brings out this point. The attorney rested his plea on the trustworthiness of the king. If the commitment for the imprisonment must be stated, then all would be acquainted with matters

---

[68] *Journal of the House of Commons*, I, 21 May, 1628, p. 902.

[69] *Journal of the House of Lords*, III, 17 May, 1628, p. 801.

[70] Frances H. Relf, *The Petition of Right* (Minneapolis: University of Minnesota Press, 1917), pp. 36 ff.

[71] *Journal of the House of Lords*, III, 20 May, 1628, p. 806.

[72] *I.e.*, Sir Edward Coke's speech, *Journal of the House of Lords*, III, 9 April, 1628, pp. 728-729.

[73] Relf, *The Petition of Right*, p. 63, App. B.

of state. The king will do no injustice: as *pater patriae* he cannot want affection for his children. Was it not a maxim at law
that "the king can do no wrong"? If he does wrong, "there is a
greater than He, the King of Kings: *respondet superiori*." [74]
Yet the Parliament wanted to control the king in this respect
and not to leave this function to a powerful but remote deity.
Such arguments were sadly out of date in 1628. The argument
that the king can do no wrong the Commons answered by care-
fully distinguishing between the office of the king and a king
"ill advised." [75] Again the Commons stated that it was not its
intention to call the king's power in question, "but to regulate
it." [76] Here we have the crux of the whole matter.

Frances Relf has given us a detailed account of Parliament's
attempt to produce a document which would be enforceable
in the courts of justice and therefore be equivalent to a law. In
the end this quest made the Petition of Right a unique document in the annals of parliamentary procedure. [77] This attempt
at enforcement, as far as the courts of justice were concerned,
is of prime importance for our argument. It is another link between the idea of regulating, and usurping, part of the prerogative and Parliament's quest for sovereignty. For this problem
brings out the point that it was not against the king alone that
Parliament had to fight for supremacy, but against the courts
as well, a problem to which we will return presently. It is for
this reason that Parliament was not satisfied with Charles's
vague answer, which merely confirmed Magna Carta. [78] The
idea of regulating the prerogative implied something more
specific. As early as 1625 Coke had said prophetically, "... when
complaint is that a grievance is against the law, it is no answer

[74] *Journal of the House of Lords*, III, 19 April, 1628, pp. 757, 758.

[75] The Commons was afraid that Buckingham was behind the king's vague
first answer to the Petition. Relf, *The Petition of Right*, p. 50.

[76] *Journal of the House of Lords*, III, 19 April, 1628, p. 759.

[77] Relf, *The Petition of Right*, III.

[78] For Charles's affirmation, see *Journal of the House of Lords*, III, 28 April
1628, p. 772.

to say [that] it shall be limited." [79] Charles was thus forced to give a specific reply.

On the whole, the Parliament was successful in enforcing the Petition in the law courts. [80] Yet the question of reason of state and the king's executive powers was not settled. Indeed, it was not to be settled until Parliament claimed in 1641 power over the army itself. Regulation without force behind it was to be of little avail. However, for our purposes, the Petition is another milestone on Parliament's road to sovereignty. Any idea of matter of state resting in a king who could do no wrong and who was appointed by God was openly rejected. An attempt was made to "regulate" this royal prerogative. Indeed, in a manner of speaking, this whole prerogative was out of date, "Because this [Parliament] a council of state, for our countries, which hath trusted us wherewith fit to be acquainted." [81]

What more startling sign of the times and the feeling of Parliament could be cited than article 3 of the indictment brought against the royalist divine, Roger Maynwaring, in 1628—just when the Petition of Right was under consideration? Maynwaring had rashly and falsely stated "that the subject hath property of his goods in ordinary; but in extraordinaries, the property was in the King." [82] Had the men who censured him read their Fortescue? There was in truth no precedent nor justification for this charge. But Maynwaring had forgotten that in the year 1628 to hold the idea of the divinity of kings was a political offense, just as the misguided Mr. Shepherd had to be taught, in 1621, that to advocate punishment for the Puritans meant sequestration from the Parliament. If these signs of the times are taken together with Parliament's actions in for-

---

[79] *Parliamentary Debates*, 1625, ed. Gardiner (1873), p. 41. For a similar statement by the Commons in 1626 see *Journal of the House of Commons*, I, 24 May, 1626, p. 863.

[80] Relf, *The Petition of Right*, pp. 57, 58.

[81] *Journal of the House of Commons*, I, 7 December, 1621, p. 659.

[82] *Journal of the House of Lords*, III, 11 June, 1628, p. 848.

eign affairs, can there be any question that Parliament had embarked on the quest for sovereignty? Or that Whitelocke's analysis had only been the beginning of a momentous development?

VII

PARLIAMENT AND THE POWER TO MAKE LAW

†

THE STRUGGLE FOR SOVEREIGNTY on the part of Parliament was bound to embrace Bodin's chief mark of a sovereign: the power to make law. In this vital area the king was not so great an obstacle to parliamentary supremacy as were the king's courts.

Relatively little has as yet been said of the limitations placed on Parliament by the common law and the judges, though we have seen the attempt to avoid judicial digression in the matter of the Petition of Right. There were the elements of a conflict between the statutory powers of Parliament and the interpretive powers of the judges, although there was, as we shall see, still a large amount of identification between judicial and legislative actions.[1] Conflict occurred largely over the matter of interpretation in those areas where the judges had no statutes to guide them. But it must be borne in mind that the power of parliamentary statutes had been recognized as binding as far back as the Year Books: we have cited above Fortescue's opin-

[1] C. H. McIlwain, *The High Court of Parliament etc.* (New Haven: Yale University Press, 1934), p. 148. Coke, for example, "never recognized the antitheses between legislation and adjudication by which the moderns have interpreted him."

ions on the power of an act of Parliament.[2] The dispute was
not a matter of principle, but of degree.

If it was true, then, that James and Charles had to fight
against the independent interpretations of the judges, so had
Parliament. Legislative sovereignty could not be fully attained
so long as the judges played "the Chancellor's part upon the
statutes." Parliament's battle for the separation of judges from
royal control was not supposed to free the judges from parliamentary control as well, and indeed, was meant to impose it.
"No judge nor any other shall presume to expound the law
contrary to the meaning of the law makers." [3]

The judges were apt to interpret laws for the benefit of the
king.

> The judges that heretofore told us, that the laws made upon so
> good ground touching Purveyors cannot bind the Prerogative;
> will they not also tell us That our Law for restrictions (on the Post
> Nati) will not bind the Prerogative? [4]

Here indeed was a very real threat to Parliament's legislative
powers, more real in a sense than that from the king, who professed never to make laws without the three estates. What, for
example, if the judges refused to hear evidence against Jesuit
priests? In 1629, the judges did just that. The Lord Chief Justice was called upon to account before the House for this stay
of justice. "Never was there the like example or precedent; if
the judges give us no better satisfaction, they themselves will
also be parties." [5] All that the men in the House could answer
to such liberties on the part of the judges was that "what answer so ever the judges return, it cannot prejudice us; the law

[2] *Vide supra*, chap. iii, and also *A Discourse upon the Statutes*, ed. S. E.
Thorne (San Marino: Huntington Library, 1942), p. 14. Talking about the
early fourteenth century, ". . . since Parliament was the highest court of the
realm its judgment was the highest record in the law. . . ."

[3] *Parliamentary Debates*, 1610, ed. S. R. Gardiner (Camden Society, 1879),
pp. 142, 143.

[4] *Parliamentary Diary of Robert Bowyer*, ed. D. H. Willson (Minneapolis:
University of Minnesota Press, 1932), pp. 265, 266.

[5] *Commons Debates*, 1629, ed. Notestein and Relf (Minneapolis: University of Minnesota Press, 1921), p. 80.

speaks by record, and if these records remain, it will to pos-
terity explain the law." [6]

Earlier, in Bates's case, the House had indulged in a full-
fledged attack on the judges for upholding the hated impositions. Attorney Hobart here touched on the fundamental issues
underlying the conflict between the legislative and judicial
powers: "If Judges may judge impositions by legal power,
then the absolute power is controllable by the legal power." [7]
Hobart to be sure was thinking of the king's absolute powers,
but to men like Whitelocke, who urged Parliament's side in
the same case, absolute power meant the power of the King in
Parliament. Again and again we find attacks on the judges for
thwarting Parliament's will. "The Judges are Judges of the
Law, not of the Parliament. God forbid the state of the Kingdom should come under the sentence of a Judge!" [8]

Members of Parliament thus realized that "for the judges to
undermine (the) privilege of Parliament were to supersede and
make void the law." [9] But that is just what the judges, under
the pressure from the king, were likely to do. Sir Edward
Coke's suggestion that Parliament might itself proceed against
corrupt judges, though embellished with precedents drawn
from the time before the Conquest, including King Alfred
(who had hanged four judges), was as futile as it was weak
in argument.[10] About attempts to reform the courts we shall
speak later. Such efforts were as a rule directed against the
courts of equity only, although the Commons made special
plans to receive petitions on the abuses of the courts in general.[11]

It was by stressing its nature as the High Court of the realm
that Parliament was, in a measure, able to assert the supremacy

[6] *Ibid.*, p. 62.

[7] *Parliamentary Debates, 1610*, ed. Gardiner (1879), p. 120.

[8] *Commons Debates, 1621*, ed. Notestein, Relf, Simpson (New Haven:
Yale University Press, 1935), II, 411.

[9] *Commons Debates, 1629*, ed. Notestein and Relf, p. 88.

[10] *Commons Debates, 1621*, ed. Notestein, Relf, Simpson, IV, 248-249.

[11] *Ibid.*, II, 207.

of its statutes. The upholding of Parliament's claims over
property was based, as we saw, on the fact that the Statute of
Uses was a "judgment" in Parliament against abuses.[12] Indeed,
though ever since the time of Sir Thomas Smith the idea of the
"making of law" by a legislative body had been accepted even
by men like Coke,[13] there were still evidences that the old ideas
lingered on. "Without judicature," said Glanville in 1621, "we
cannot make laws, therefore we must use judicature." [14]
"Every man that sits here is a judge," exclaimed Coke.[15] Parliament is the "highest and most honorable and absolute court of
justice in England." [16] Parliament thus claimed the judicial
"highest appeal" to go hand in hand with its claim to legislative sovereignty. But a judgment of the whole Parliament
other than by impeachment was in the form of a statute. Only
the House of Lords was a court of judgment proper.[17] This
fact was asserted most strikingly in Floyd's case. Here the
Commons tried to use its function as part of the High Court
to enforce its wishes and to punish its enemies. Floyd had
attacked the "palsgrave," whose cause the House of Commons, at least, was supporting. It was at this point that the
House decided to push to its furthest extent its judicial pretensions, to use them as sanctions to enforce its will. It attempted
to punish Floyd without recourse to the Lords. Even Coke had
to admit that, in passing judgment on Floyd without consulting the Lords, the House had outrun its functions.[18] He was
here in agreement with James. In the end one member proposed
to settle this vexing question by passing a bill to condemn
Floyd.[19] Here again we have the tacit admission that the ordi-

[12] *Vide supra*, chap. iii.
[13] Sir Edward Coke, *Second Institutes* (London, 1797), pt. I, 157.
[14] *Commons Debates*, 1621, ed. Notestein, Relf, Simpson, II, 532.
[15] *Ibid.*, II, 233.
[16] Sir Edward Coke, *First Institutes* (London, 1794), chap. 10, sect. 164, lib. 2.
[17] *I.e.*, *Parliamentary Diary of Robert Bowyer*, p. 214. In 1606 the Lords
replied to the Commons: "Next they do not conceive that this house doth
make a Court, but that both houses together make one Court."
[18] *Commons Debates*, 1621, ed. Notestein, Relf, Simpson, II, 362.
[19] *Ibid.*, II, 340.

nary course of judgment by Parliament as a whole was by bill.
If it was asserted in 1614 that "noble men have been punished
by the lower house," [20] it would have been the old process of
impeachment that was being brought to light again as, indeed,
it was in 1621, to be used against the monopolist Mompesson.

The term "High Court of Parliament," then, did not mean
that the House of Commons alone could use its power of judicature to enforce its will on those who were not its members.
From the point of view of the Commons, its powers were
confined in this respect to indictments before the Lords and to
acts of Parliament to be passed also by the Lords and approved by the king. The sovereign powers of "last appeal" and
of the making of law applied to the whole of Parliament. In
this sense the quest for parliamentary sovereignty must be distinguished from the gaining of the initiative of the House of
Commons alone.

Of the power and jurisdiction of Parliament for making of laws
in proceeding by bill, it is so trandescendent and absolute, as it
cannot be confined either to persons or causes within any bounds.[21]

And a bill required the assent of the Lords as well as of the king.
And yet there were cases when the judgment of the High
Court of Parliament was questioned by the lawyers and courts,
despite this sweeping statement by Coke. It was not merely in
the case of staying justice or of pro-royalist interpretations, for
it was when there were no clearly worded statutes to guide
them that the judges were apt to assert their role in the constitution.

The law, James held, must be interpreted according to the
meaning and not according to its literal sense: *"nam ratio est
anima legis."* [22] This assertion was endorsed by no less a person
than Coke himself. For example, the time when a statute was

[20] *Ibid.,* VII, 630.

[21] Sir Edward Coke, *Fourth Institutes* (London, 1797), p. 36.

[22] "Basilikon Doron," *Political Works of James I,* ed. C. H. McIlwain (Cambridge, Mass.: Harvard University Press, 1918), p. 38.

made has to be taken into consideration by the judges, for *"distinguenda sunt tempora."* [23]

Lord Chancellor Ellesmere, too, justified judicial interpretations in a similar manner, for all human laws were but *"leges temporia."* Though they might be meant for the times in which they were made, new times might demand changes.[24] This idea in itself allows for broadness of interpretations, and both royalist judges and Coke seem to have concurred on this point. This concept was again strikingly stated by Justice Hobart:

> If you ask me: then, by what rules judges guided themselves? . . . [I answer] by that liberty and authority judges have over laws . . . to mold them to the truest and best use.[25]

But we must add here one all-important factor which does not come to light in Justice Hobart's dicta, namely the frequent assumption that all acts of Parliament must, by the very fact that they are such acts, be reasonable. Again here we can go back to St. Germain's dictum that no act of Parliament will recite anything against the truth.[26] As a member of Parliament put it, "All Law is reason, but not all reason Law. . . . Acts of Parliament [are] reasonable, but no Laws till they be made." [27] Thus an interpretation of the Statute of Uses was justified in the following manner: "It is reasonable in regard of every subject who are parties or privies to the act of Parliament that it should not turn to the prejudice of any. For an act of Law shall prejudice no man." [28] Sir John Eliot, in an effort to pass a new bill to disinherit spurious sons, attacked the older legislation on the grounds that "though the letter of the law doth approve it,

[23] Sir Edward Coke, *Reports etc.* (Edinburgh, 1907), LXXVI, 53, Porter's Case.

[24] Case of Post Nati, *State Trials etc.*, ed. T. Howell (London, 1809), p. 674.

[25] Theodore Plucknett, "Bonham's Case and Judicial Review," *Harvard Law Review*, XL (November, 1926), 50.

[26] *Vide supra*, chap. i.

[27] Hedley, in *Parliamentary Debates*, 1610, ed. Gardiner (1879), pp. 72, 73.

[28] Coke, *Reports etc.*, LXXVII, 359, Sir Moyle Finch's Case.

the reason of the law does deny it." [29] Therefore he implied
that the old law was not valid law.

Here indeed the idea of reason provided a ready weapon for
judicial interpretations, as the law of nature had done of old.
Acts of Parliament were the highest law of the land, to be sure,
but they had to stay within the bounds of reason. On the other
hand, there was a presupposition of reasonableness concerning
the acts of Parliament—and, if they should not be in conformity with reason, judicial interpretation should endeavor to
make them conform. If, for example, an act of Parliament
decreed a punishment and the offender against the act had
offended in spite of his own will, the judges should acquit him.

For it would be unreasonable that those things which are inevitable by act of God, which no industry can avoid nor policy prevent, should be construed to the prejudice of any person. . . .[30]

The idea of reasonableness here comes close to the idea of repugnancy of matters unable to be performed. This is no doubt
what Coke had in mind when he wrote that "In 9H.4 an act
of Parliament was made which was absolutely *in terrorem* and
was utterly against the Law," namely the expulsion of all Irish
from England.[31]

The law, being reasonable, can never be the occasion for
outright wrong.[32] But then, acts of Parliament must be reasonable by the very fact that they were made by Parliament—
at least, Parliament must have meant them to be in conformity
with reason. Whether we have here an idea of a superior law
like the medieval law of nature we must leave until we have
examined the nature of this "reason" somewhat closer. From
the point of view of Parliament's quest for legislative sovereignty, this idea of judicial freedom was as dangerous as it was
to James himself. To what lengths this judicial interpretation

[29] John Foster, *Sir John Eliot* (London, 1872), p. 77, Duncombe's Case.
[30] Coke, *Reports etc.*, LXXVI, 219, Shelley's Case.
[31] *State Trials etc.*, II, 726.
[32] Coke, *Reports etc.*, LXXVII, 99, Coulter's Case.

could go is illustrated when we contemplate Justice Dalton's statement on the matter of contracts. In contracts between masters and apprentices, "and all other covenants, *conventio legem vincit.*" And Dalton, too, believed strongly that this was grounded, like all law, on reason.[33]

Would it be too much to see in this matter of judicial interpretation the great stumbling block to Parliament's attainment of full legislative sovereignty? Was it perhaps the judges more than the king who defeated Parliament's claims in this direction? True, royal proclamations could still be regarded by some as positive law. But could the judges, by twisting acts of Parliament into the strait jacket of their idea of "reasonableness," not work even greater havoc with the desires of Parliament? All the arguments of Parliament as custodian of the common good would not prevail in such matters as Bates's case where there was no specific act of Parliament to guide the judges. It was, in a manner of speaking, *pro bono publico* that according to reason an act of Parliament "should not prejudice the inheritance of any"; should not ask things impossible to be performed, such as the expulsion of the Irish; should not punish a person for acts for which he was not responsible.

Coke's words about the power of Parliament must, therefore, be modified.

The jurisdiction of the court [of Parliament] is so transcendent, that it maketh, enlargeth, abrogateth, repealeth and reviveth laws, statutes, acts, ordinances, concerning matters ecclesiastical, criminal, canon, civil, martial, maritime, and the rest.[34]

While the idea of *pro bono publico* did not avail against the judges, it did prove effective against the legislative pretentions of the king. Coke held that "The King being head of the Commonwealth, cannot be an instrument to defeat the purview of an act of Parliament made *pro bono publico.*"[35] On another occasion Coke put it in slightly different form: "Acts against

[33] Michael Dalton, *The Justice of the Peace etc.* (London, 1746), p. 135.
[34] Sir Edward Coke, *First Institutes* (London, 1749), chap. x, sect. 164, lib. 2.
[35] Coke, *Reports etc.*, LXXVII, 71, Case of Ecclesiastical Persons.

the power of Parliament subsequently bind not." The king cannot grant exemption to any man to be freed from election to Parliament,

because elections to them ought to be free and his attendance is for the service of the whole realm, and for the benefit of the king and his people, and the whole commonwealth hath an interest therein.[36]

Here the idea of representation was combined with the idea of the common interest. Indeed these two concepts were closely allied. It is no coincidence that the pamphleteer who wrote, citing Sir Thomas Smith, that the authority of Parliament is absolute and binds all manners of persons, should go on to remark that this is the case because all men are a party to Parliament's actions.[37]

The attack on the king's powers to legislate by proclamation demonstrates once again the use of the idea *pro bono publico* against the king. Indeed, when Coke penned his phrase, cited above, it was against James's protection of monopolies by proclamation that he was protesting. Coke held that no royal proclamation should go out for private causes. A proclamation must be *pro bono publico*, not *privato*.[38] The implication here seems clear. The king could make proclamation for the public good, but an act of Parliament *pro bono publico* had a higher authority than any proclamation issued for reason of state. Protesting against a proclamation concerning the observance of Lent, Alford queried, "We sit here in Parliament to make laws, where our ancestors have sat who have made laws that we are governed by and not by proclamations. . . . And shall proclama-

---

[36] Coke, *Fourth Institutes*, p. 48.

[37] Thomas Powell, *The Attourneys Academy etc.* (London, 1623), p. 220. See also *Parliamentary Diary of Robert Bowyer*, p. 97 ". . . Yea all the Realme is intended present. . . ." (Robert Bowyer). See Miss Judson's excellent account of representation, *The Crisis of the Constitution* (New Brunswick: Rutgers University Press, 1949), pp. 274 ff.

[38] *Commons Debates*, 1621, ed. Notestein, Relf, Simpson, II, 118-119.

tions make laws of no effect?" [39] Nominally at least, the issue of proclamations as separate law had already been settled in the reign of Henry VIII, for despite his efforts to widen the scope of proclamations, Parliament had given him only such power of proclamation as did not conflict with the law of the land and the property rights of the subject.[40] The importance of this new attack on proclamations consists in that it tended once again to restrict the king in his sphere of influence. Alford protested against a proclamation on ecclesiastical affairs not in tune with Puritan precepts.[41] In 1621 the House protested a proclamation regarding the exportation of ordnance to Spain, a matter of foreign policy.

A good deal of the struggle against proclamation was, of course, waged over the matter of parliamentary privileges. The liberty of the House, asserted Coke, was like a circle, if any part of it be broken, "the whole is broken for no proclamation can be in force against an Act of Parliament." [42] But we are here not so much concerned with the Parliament's struggle for internal independence, though this struggle was a vital prerequisite to the actual enforcement of its claims when the time came.[43]

[39] *Ibid.*, p. 120. See also Alford's remark, "That liberty of speeche was taken away by the Proclamacion and this high Courte made subject to the Counsell Table," *ibid.*, IV, 433.

[40] For Statute of Proclamation see *Sources of English Constitutional History*, ed. Carl Stephenson and F. G. Marcham (New York: Harper & Bros., 1937), pp. 316-317.

[41] *Commons Debates, 1621,* ed. Notestein, Relf, Simpson, IV, 432-433.

[42] *Ibid.*, II, 22.

[43] This has been treated by Carl Wittke, *The History of English Parliamentary Privilege* (Columbus: The Ohio State University Press, 1921). Dr. Wittke says little about such matters as the Commons' attempt to dispute the king's power in summoning and dissolving Parliament. Alford, for example, denied that the king could break up the house before things at hand are disposed of. *Commons Debates and Proceedings,* 1620 and 1621, ed. E. Nicholas (Oxford, 1766), p. 119. Coke held that the king could begin, continue, and end Parliament at his pleasure. *Commons Debates, 1621,* ed. Notestein, Relf, Simpson, II, 403. Hakewill sought a compromise by which the king might dissolve the Parliament while it might adjourn itself; *ibid.*, II, 420.

In matters of commerce and trade, however, the battle over proclamations was fought most bitterly. It was to a great extent connected with the struggle against monopolies. Indeed, throughout the debates about the king's power of proclamation there seems to have been the feeling that the issue of monopolies itself was more important than the power of proclamation *per se*.[44] To this there was added also the feeling that proclamations were open to almost any abuse in the matter of fines. "In law the penalty is known, in proclamations the mult is uncertain."[45] At last, in 1624, by the Statute of Monopolies, the king's powers in this regard were severely curbed.[46] Yet as late as 1623 it could be stated that proclamations were positive law, just as were acts of Parliament. "Proclamations are where the king and his council think fit and expedient to publish anything as a law." And this "according to the common received opinion"![47] These brief examples may serve to demonstrate the use of the ideas of common good and of representation against the king's legislative powers.

It seems clear that Parliament in its way had gone far beyond the idea of *droit gouvernement*, in much the same way as the royalists had done in their turn. Both claimed the right to control the property of private persons, the right to make laws, the attributes of government such as control over war and peace. But with both, too, the common law seemed to stand as a bar to the acquisition of complete sovereignty. The idea of sovereignty had surely been assimilated to a great degree in the English commonwealth. Sir Thomas Smith would have been surprised to see it stated as consciously as Whitelocke did. Well might James compare members of Parliament to "Children which if they have not one thing will have nothing."[48]

---

[44] *Ibid.*, pp. 121, 124, 125. See, for example, the different opinions about proclamations of Glanville, Crewe, and Nay.

[45] *Ibid.*, IV, 90.

[46] For a discussion of this statute see D. L. Keir, *Constitutional History of Modern Britain* (London: A. & C. Black, 1938), p. 167.

[47] Powell, *The Attourneys Academy etc.*, p. 225.

[48] *Commons Debates, 1621*, ed. Notestein, Relf, Simpson, VII, 647.

Charles I, looking back over the Parliament of 1628, was moved to proclaim:

We are not ignorant how much the House hath of late years endeavored to expand their privilege by setting up general committees for religion, for courts of justice, for trade and the like: a course never heard of until late; so that where in former times the Knights and Burgesses were wont to communicate to the House such business as they brought from their countries, now there are so many chairs erected to make inquiry upon all sorts of men . . . to the unsufferable disturbance and scandal of justice and government; which having been tolerated awhile by Our father and our Self hath daily grown to more and more height . . . their drift was, by this means to break through all respects and ligaments of government, and to erect a universal overswaying power to themselves, which belongs only to us and not to them.[49]

Charles's analysis of Parliament's quest for sovereignty was certainly not wide of the mark, but his conclusion may stand typical for the mutual quest for complete sovereignty by both the king and the Parliament. The overswaying power traditionally belonged to neither exclusively, but to both, knit together *in dominium politicum et regale*. By 1629 the struggle for sovereignty was to enter a more violent phase leading eventually to the field of battle. That same year Charles issued another proclamation concerning his late Parliament. He was forced to contradict the rumor that Eliot's resolutions, re-enforcing the Petition of Right, had been voted by the entire House of Commons. Charles, further, had to admit that by this rumor trade was being disrupted and merchants were being discouraged from pursuing their trade. While promising to levy no other duties than those his father had levied before him, the king went on to forbid any discussion of future meetings of the Parliament. The late advances by the Commons had, for the present, driven him from contemplating another meet-

[49] *Royal Proclamation* (London, 1628), pp. 6, 33-34. For a justification of Charles see Harold P. Cooke, *Charles I and his Early Parliaments* (London: The Sleldon Press, 1939).

ing.[50] The battle lines were thus being drawn ever more firmly. By the 1630's many an Englishman must have disagreed with the lines written by a devoted royalist: "Is any land or any clime more blest than Britain at this time?" [51] Yet throughout the struggle for sovereignty there were still men, common lawyers like Sir Edward Coke, who, in the name of the law of reason or of nature, were attempting to restore the balance of the constitution, who attempted to deny "sovereignty" and to stress "harmony" in the medieval manner. To their quest, and to their dilemma, we now turn.

[50] *A Proclamation for suppressing of false Rumors touching Parliament* (London, 1629).

[51] P. M., *King Charles, his Birthright* (Edinburgh, 1633).

VIII

COMMON LAW AND SOVEREIGNTY

I

THE QUEST FOR SOVEREIGNTY by both king and Parliament undermined concepts of natural law, a development extending
from the Tudor period. In the fifteenth century, Sir John Fortescue still believed that the law of nature defined "property"
on the one hand, and the limits of authority on the other. We
have noted the absence of all natural law in the thought of Sir
Thomas Smith at the end of the Tudor period and have seen
that even the courts began to accept by then the idea of Parliament's power to change the property of private men. Perhaps
the weakening of this natural law was symbolized by St. Germain's concept of the law of reason, but even the law of reason,
as it was described by Hooker, no longer protected property
from the growing power of the community as a whole.

Yet the idea of a "higher" law still played a most important
part as a bar to sovereignty in the first half of the seventeenth
century. We have seen how the idea of "reason" provided a
ready weapon for the judicial interpretation of parliamentary
statutes. It is this concept and its relationship to the common
law that is here subject to a closer analysis.

One phrase was held in common by both Sir Edwin Sandys

and the Lord Chancellor Ellesmere. Ellesmere contended: *"Deficiente lege recurritur ad consuetudinem, deficiente consuetudine recurritur ad rationem naturalem."* [1] What is the meaning of this *rationem naturalem?* And what in turn did Coke mean when he repeated with approval Littleton's dictum that *"ratio est anima legis"?* [2] These phrases must have been more than mere ornaments destined for the ears of continental jurists. Perhaps "reason" was even a more specific concept than merely the "living embodiment of the collective reason of mankind." [3]

Justice Dalton began,

> The common laws of this realm of England, receiving principally their grounds from the laws of God and nature (which law of nature, as it pertaineth to man) is also called the law of reason,

and went on to refer to Fortescue's *De Laudibus.* Here again we can read about the universality of the law of nature, from whose principle many of the maxims of the common law are themselves deduced. [4] Was this law of reason then a sort of higher law, as the law of nature had been to Sir John Fortescue? Even as late as 1627, Sir Henrie Finch spoke of the law of reason as the "higher and more perfect law" before which positive laws should give way. [5] Fullbeck held that if there were two contradictory laws, that law should be followed which is most in conformity with the laws of reason. [6] Both Sandys and Ellesmere, as we saw, seemed to treat the *rationalem naturalem* as a kind of last appeal. Coke, too, seemed to take a similar stand when

---

[1] Ellesmere in the Case of Post Nati, *State Trials etc.,* ed. T. Howell (London, 1809), II, 672. Sandys in *Commons Debates,* 1621, ed. Notestein, Relf, Simpson, (New Haven: Yale University Press, 1935), II, 349. See also Hakewill: "There was no precedent in the case so that now we are left to reason." *Ibid.,* IV, 54.

[2] Sir Edward Coke, *First Institutes* (London, 1794), II, Epilogue.

[3] Sir Frederick Pollock, *Essays in the Law* (London: Macmillan, 1922), p. 128.

[4] Michael Dalton, *The Justice of the Peace etc.* (London, 1746), I, citing Sir John Fortescue, *De Laudibus Legem Angliae,* chap. xvii.

[5] Sir Henrie Finch, *Law or a Discourse Thereof etc.* (London, 1796), pp. 4-6.

[6] *Vide supra,* p. 34 ff.

he implied that law has to be approved by "authority and reason."[7]

The common law was constantly being identified with this "higher and more perfect law." Sir John Doderidge toward 1620 wrote of the common law that it was "often styled in our books common reason."[8] Bacon cited Fitzherbert's dictum that "Common reason is common law."[9] This partial identification of the common law and the law of reason is of primary importance, for it could serve the common law as protective armor against encroachments of all other jurisdictions. How could the law of reason be known by man? When Lord Chancellor Ellesmere felt himself forced to *recurrere ad rationem*, other examples and arguments having failed him, he expressly rejected the idea that reason might be the "light and distempered reasons of common discoursers: drowned with drink or blown away with a whiff of tobacco." Instead there should be gravity, learning, experience, and authority, for only by study and labor might a man acquire knowledge of the law of reason.[10]

There is here none of the eighteenth-century concept of reason as a boon given naturally to every human being. The emphasis of common lawyers was placed on study and learning as the only road to proper reason and the comprehension of the higher law. In 1625 the Lord Keeper admonished the students of law to bend their studies to the ancient maxims of law, where they would find the ancient grounds of law, founded in reason and proceeding from God himself. True, he was here arguing against the common law, which he believed issued only from the inventions of men.[11] But the emphasis was nevertheless on learning and study, on delving into the origins of the law. How easily might such an argument be turned in favor of common law itself! Even Fleming implicitly admitted that reason was

[7] Coke, *First Institutes*, XXXVI, Preface.

[8] Sir John Doderidge, *The English Lawyer* (London, 1631), p. 62.

[9] Sir Francis Bacon, "Reading on the Statute of Uses," *Works of Sir Francis Bacon*, ed. Spedding and Heath (London, 1892), VII, 415.

[10] Case of Post Nati, *State Trials etc.*, II, 686.

[11] *Parliamentary Debates*, 1625, ed. S. R. Gardiner (Camden Society, 1873), pp. 4, 5.

extracted from books of law, for (in Bates's case) he pointed out explicitly that his reasons did not come from books of law but were based on policy. These reasons of policy he justified in turn by pointing out their very antiquity.[12] Even royalist lawyers seemed to have identified the law of reason with learning and study centering on the ancient practices of the realm. In this way it approached the older concept of the natural law, for as the common lawyer used the term "law of reason," it could serve as a shield against the encroachment of sovereign power.

It was Coke who gave the perfect expression to this concept of "legal reason."

And by reasoning and debating of grave learned men the darkness of ignorance is expelled, and by the light of legal reason the right is discerned, and thereupon judgment given according to law, which is the perfection of reason. This is of Littleton here called *legitima ratio*, whereupon no man can attain but by long study, often conference, long experience, and continual observation.[13]

He would have agreed with Doderidge's brief definition of the law:

A rule or principle of the law of England, is a conclusion either of the law of nature, or derived from general custom used within the realm, containing in a short sum the reason or direction of many particular or special occurrences.[14]

The process of law, then, was always the deduction of the particular from the general, the general maxim being founded on common reason.[15] Coke, too, commended the student of law first to acquaint himself with the reason of the law, which was the life of the law, before going on to understand particular cases.[16]

The idea of the law of reason was here by no means merely an ornament. In Coke's view as well as in Doderidge's, as we have seen, legal reason was a concept open only to those who

[12] Bates's Case, *State Trials etc.*, II, 388.
[13] Coke, *First Institutes*, chap. v, sect. 377, lib. 3.
[14] Doderidge, *The English Lawyer*, p. 153.
[15] *Ibid.*, p. 93.
[16] Coke, *First Institutes*, chap. iii, sect. 283, lib. 3.

had studied the maxims of the law, to those who had read the *Institutes* or were acquainted with the *English Lawyer*. Sir Henrie Finch enlarged here in an interesting manner: common reason, that is to say, the common law, was not everybody's reason. It was "refined" reason generally received by the consent of all.[17] He may here have been thinking not only of custom but also of acts of Parliament as the receptacle of refined reason. That there was always a presumption that acts of Parliament were in conformity with reason we have seen above. But it was those trained in "legal reason" who decided this. At one point the judges condescendingly referred to part of a statute as being inserted rather to satisfy some of the burgesses in Parliament who were "ignorant in the laws" than for any necessity.[18] The presumption that the law of reason was in the hands of the lawyers was of prime importance, for this made them in a sense arbiters not only of the king's actions but of acts of Parliament as well. It enabled the common lawyers to be the great obstacle in the path of the acquisition of sovereignty in the constitution. In a manner of speaking, it substituted their learning for the "divinity" which had in the past removed the law of nature from arbitrary interference.

What did the concept "reason" mean when applied to the statutes of a Parliament that was, in Coke's own words, the "Highest Court in England"? We have touched on this subject in discussing the possible area of conflict between statute and common law. The question seems to be bound up with Ellesmere's dictum that "a thing repugnant is void." [19] Coke cited the invalidation of an act exiling the Irish from England because it was absolutely "*in terrorem*." [20] The Statute of Uses was

[17] Finch, *Law or a Discourse Thereof etc.*, p. 75.

[18] Sir Edward Coke, *Reports etc.* (Edinburgh, 1907), pp. 54, 76, Porter's Case.

[19] Ellesmere's tract on Statutes quoted in S. E. Thorne, "The Constitution and the Courts, A Re-examination of the Famous Case of Dr. Bonham," *The Constitution Reconsidered*, ed. Conyers Read (New York: Columbia University Press, 1938), p. 22.

[20] Case of Proclamations, *State Trials etc.*, II, 726.

modified because "an act in law shall prejudice no man." [21]
Still more to the point was the decision of the judges in a case
where a man would have been his own executor in the matter
of debts.

> And it is not reasonable that one should take advantage of his
> own wrong, and if the law should give him such power, the law
> would be the cause and the occasion of wrong . . . and the law of
> God says: no facias malum. . . .[22]

We have the idea again presented by the judges when they said
on another occasion, "An act of Parliament to which everyone
is party can do no wrong." [23] And the judges made certain that
the act of Parliament did not defeat its purpose.

It is here that the famous case of Bonham, wherein Coke
seemed to revoke an act of Parliament, is significant. It was
against reason that a man should be made a judge in his own
case.[24] This need hardly astonish us. Was not Coke's whole case
against the king's judicial pretensions built in turn on the idea
that the "King cannot be judge in his own case"? [25] Dr. Thorne
seems to be correct when he calls Coke's judgment in Bonham's
case a mere expression of repugnancy. Yet this repugnancy was
justified by an appeal to the law of reason.

Too little attention has been paid in this connection to Coke's
justification of his own decision. On the king's behalf, Lord
Chancellor Ellesmere had, among other things, accused Coke
of going too far in the matter of judicial discretion. Coke answered by showing that other acts of Parliament had been
annulled in common law courts when they were against com-

---

[21] Coke, *Reports etc.*, LXVII, 77, 359, Sir Moyle Finch's Case.

[22] *Ibid.*, pp. 77, 99, Coulter's Case.

[23] *Ibid.*, pp. 77, 294, Viscount Montague's Case.

[24] For a discussion of this case see S. E. Thorne, in *The Constitution Recon-sidered*, ed. Conyers Read. See also Thorne's edition of *A Discourse upon the Statutes etc.* (San Marino: Huntington Library, 1942), pp. 85, 92. See also Theodore Plucknett, "Bonham's Case and Judicial Review," *Harvard Law Review*, 40, pp. 30-70.

[25] See Sir Edward Coke in *Commons Debates*, 1621, ed. Notestein, Relf, Simpson, II, 195.

mon right and reason. He cited a part of the Statute of Carlisle: the common seal of the Cistercians and Augustines should be in the custody of the prior, who was under the abbott, and of four others of the house, and any deed sealed with a seal not so kept was to be void. This clause was to be rejected, said Coke, because it was impertinent to be observed: the seal being in the custody of those mentioned above, the abbott could not seal anything with it, for when he had it, it was *ipso facto* out of their custody.[26]

Coke's opinion in Bonham's case was harmonious with the whole idea of "legal reason." But could this idea as expressed in Bonham's case have been an idea of superior right only when read "in the light of St. Germain's and Fortescue's natural law"? [27] Must we not indeed read the idea of "reason" in just this light? Here, too, was the protective element which we have seen operating in the earlier natural law regarding property. An act of Parliament could dispose of property, but in all other instances the reason of the law insured the certainty of possession, and even an act of Parliament could be modified in the light of the law of reason.

We have cited examples to this effect in the last chapter; others could be added. For example, the courts held a proviso of an act of Parliament illegal because it included "words uncertain and void in law, and God forbid that the inheritances and estates of men should depend upon such uncertainty." [28] At another time the judges held that

. . . every man by the law of God, of nature, and of nations, was bound to provide a competent living for his wife, his children, and for the payments of his debts.

[26] "The Humble and Direct Answer to the Fourth Question Arising out of Dr. Bonham's Case," *Works of Sir Francis Bacon,* ed. Basil Montagu (London, 1827), VII, 375.

[27] Asserted by S. E. Thorne, in *The Constitution Reconsidered,* ed. Conyers Read, p. 23. See also Thorne's discussion of the case in *A Discourse upon the Statutes* (Marino: Huntington Library, 1942), pp. 85-92.

[28] Coke, *Reports etc.,* LXXVII, 316, Sir Anthony Mildmay's Case.

Therefore land could not be devised from heirs to strangers.[29] This decision of the judges was a rationalization of that part of the Statute of Uses which forbade the devising of land by will. Here the law of God and reason helped the court once again to adjust itself to Parliament's power as expressed in that statute.

On the other hand, would it be too much to regard such constructions as the survivals from the medieval concept of higher law? Was not even the idea of repugnancy and contradictions based on a higher view of law and justice than the mere impossibility of enforcing the laws? Bacon stated it well:

> But if a rule be one of the higher sort of maxims, that are *regula rationales* and not *positivae*, then the law will rather endure a particular offense to escape without punishment than violate such a rule.

If an offender was by law to lose his right hand for his offense, and that hand has been cut off in wars, he shall not therefore lose his left hand, but rather go unpunished.[30] Even outside the purely legal sphere, arguments with a similar view were common. Impositions were not agreeable to reason because they were *ex diametro* opposed in the main point of their intention, the benefit of the king.[31] Allegiance, Bacon held, could be applied only to the king's person. Otherwise the king's body natural would be looked upon as a corporation. "A corporation can have no wife, nor a corporation can have no son." Such a view was contrary to the very reason of the law.[32] The higher law of reason made such repugnancies void, just as it guarded against uncertainties in matters of possession. It was a practical law, like Fortescue's law of nature. Law, says Coke, is called "right" because it was the "best birthright a sub-

---

[29] *Ibid.*, LXXVII, 371, Sir George Curson's Case.

[30] Sir Francis Bacon, "Maxims of the Law," *Works of Sir Francis Bacon,* ed. Spedding and Heath (London, 1892), VII, 360.

[31] John Forster, *Sir John Elliot* (London, 1872), p. 89.

[32] Case of Post Nati, *State Trials etc.*, ed. T. Howell (London, 1809), II, 598.

ject has: for thereby his goods, life, honour, lands, wife, etc., are protected from injury and wrong." [33]

The law of reason was in the custody of the lawyers and they saw to it that the law remained synonymous with "right." Acts of Parliament could dispose of the property of private men, but obvious repugnancies were righted in court. In the name of the law of reason the judges played the "chancellor's part upon the statutes." [34] However generally law may speak,

. . . it nevertheless must be restricted lest if reason be absent [the law] itself cease to exist. For since reason is the core and the strength [of the law] a legislator does not seem to [have] appreciated this [fact] of that law which lacks reason. However, otherwise the generality of words may at first glance suggest. [35]

And it was the judges who did the restricting.

It seems therefore likely that when Sandys and Ellesmere talked about the *rationem naturalem* they meant something definite; yet both diverged from the idea of reason as expressed by Coke. Ellesmere himself was not too far from the mark in his idea of legal reason, though he conceded to the king an important place in its interpretation. Sandys, however, identified his *rationem naturalem* with the law of nations.

With such an identification Coke could not have agreed. To him natural law and the law of nations were separate entities. Slavery, for example, did not spring out of the law of nature. It existed by the law of nations as opposed to the law of nature. [36] *Ius gentium* was to Coke simply the law of nations by which aliens were tried. [37] The *ius gentium* was for Coke too

[33] Sir Edward Coke, *Second Institutes* (London, 1797), Pt. I, 56.

[34] Ellesmere quoted in C. H. McIlwain, *The High Court of Parliament etc.* (New Haven: Yale University Press, 1934), p. 295.

[35] Sir Edward Coke, *Fourth Institutes* (London, 1797), p. 330. "Quamvis lex generaliter loquitur, restringenda tamen est, ut cessante ratione et ipsa cesset: cum enim ratio sit anima vigora; ipsuis legis non videtur legislator id sensisse, quod ratione careat, etiamsi verborum generalita prima facie aliter suadeat."

[36] Coke, *First Institutes*, chap. xi, sec. 172, lib. II.

[37] Coke, *Fourth Institutes*, p. 153.

much bound up, no doubt, with the law of Rome. An identification of *ius gentium* and *ius naturale* was therefore dangerous, just as the identification of the common law and the natural law, or law of reason, was to his advantage. It is no coincidence that Sandys went on to appeal to the Roman law against the Post Nati after identifying *ius gentium* and natural reason.[38] We have pointed out how civilians like Thomas Ridley advocated the introduction into England of Roman law because of its universality, which seemed to approximate it to the law of nature.[39]

It is the *rationem legalem* of Coke which provided the common lawyers with an ideology in opposing the king and in modifying even the statutes of Parliament, though it must be borne in mind that negative statutes were not, of course, affected. Well might James, neither trained at the Inns of Court nor deeply studied in the common law, and therefore not himself acquainted with the law of reason, sigh, "But for reason, that is so large a thing as that a man knows not where to pitch." [40]

This legal reason was, then, neither so vague as James asserted, nor merely an adorning figure of speech. Here we still have some of the continuity with the law of nature, a bar to the idea of absolute sovereignty.

Besides the idea of the law of reason, the law of God continued to appear in the writings of the lawyers. Justice Dalton, quoting St. Germain, wrote:

. . . and also if any general custom were directed against the law of God, or if any statute were made directly against it: as if it were ordained that no alms should be given for no necessity, the custom and the statute were void.[41]

---

[38] Case of Post Nati, *State Trials etc.*, II, 563.

[39] Thomas Ridley, *A View of the Civil and Ecclesiastical Law* (Oxford, 1634), p. 3.

[40] *Commons Debates*, 1621, ed. Notestein, Relf, Simpson (New Haven: Yale University Press, 1935), II, 343.

[41] Dalton, *The Justice of the Peace etc.*, p. 15.

James in his turn spoke of God's law, by which all common and municipal laws must be governed.[42] A member of Parliament asserted that it was according to both the laws of God and of reason that a laborer should have his hire.[43] Was there a distinction between the law of God and the law of reason? At times we get the supposition that the law of reason sprang out of the law of God.[44] To one writer the main maxims of the law of England seem to spring directly from the law of God. The king of England must, according to God's law, govern his kingdom by laws made with the advice of his people and molded on God's law.[45] The laws of England, however, were first fashioned after the laws of the Romans and other heathens, but "at this day" they are more agreeable to the law of God than any other law of the world.[46]

> Therefore the laws of England . . . having such affinity to the laws of God, and taking their original from them, cannot be substantially handled without first searching into the laws of God. . . .[47]

But if we continue to search for some definition of what constitutes God's law, we have to fall back upon the Scriptures and especially upon the Decalogue, which Coke also seemed to regard as the fountainhead of the law of God.

The phrase "law of God" seems to have been used vaguely, at times merely to appeal against the king's powers. "Kings ought not by the law of God thus to oppress their subjects."[48]

[42] James I, "Speech in Star Chamber 1616," *Political Works of James I*, ed. C. H. McIlwain (Cambridge, Mass.: Harvard University Press, 1918), p. 330.

[43] Sir William Fleetwood in *Commons Debates, 1621*, ed. Notestein, Relf, Simpson, IV, 373.

[44] *I.e.*, Lord Chancellor: "They should find the ancient grounds of the law founded in reason proceeding from God Himself." *Parliamentary Debates, 1625*, ed. S. R. Gardiner (Camden Society, 1873), p. 5.

[45] *The Laws of England* (n. d.) Ellesmere 34; 17, 40, 41 (Henceforth Ellesmere papers will be abbreviated El.). This tract was written in the reign of Charles I, to whom the author refers frequently and upon whom he heaps flattery.

[46] *Ibid.*, p. 1.

[47] *Ibid.*, p. 1.

[48] Mr. Coryton in *Commons Debates, 1629*, ed. Notestein and Relf (Minneapolis: University of Minnesota, 1921), p. 61.

Or again, Hoskyns referred to the seventeenth chapter of Deuteronomy to show that "there is no such power said to be in the king as that he could take the goods of the subject. . . ." [49]

Perhaps the place of the law of God in the thought of the lawyers was best expressed by Coke himself. In the *Institutes* he referred to this higher law, but never so consistently as he referred to the law of reason. Equivocation in the taking of oaths was condemned by the ancient laws of England, "and this is grounded on the law of God." [50] The law against rumors was grounded on the law of God.[51] Usury was against the laws of God and nature.[52] Here we may have a shadowy distinction between the law of God and the law of nature. It would seem that the solution of this question might lie in Coke's discussion of the keeping of brothels: "[This] is against the law of God, on which the common law of England, in that case, is grounded." [53] The presumption here seems to be that only in certain cases is the law of England grounded upon the law of God, but in Coke's opinion it was always grounded upon the law of reason. It might be added that Coke, as well as the other writers cited above, always automatically proceeded to cite chapter and verse from the Bible to prove God's law.

It seems indeed as if, for Coke at any rate, God's law was enshrined entirely in the Bible. It would, however, lead to a grave misunderstanding of Coke's whole position to attribute Puritan leanings to the great lawyer because of his reliance upon the Scriptures. In 1607 he openly stated that to do away with bishops would be to do away with Parliament as well. Amending James's famous dictum, Coke stated, ". . . if no bishops, then no laws; if no laws, no kings. . . ." [54] Here, too, Coke seems

---

[49] Mr. Hoskyns in *Parliamentary Diary of Robert Bowyer*, ed. D. H. Willson (Minneapolis: University of Minnesota Press, 1932), p. 61.

[50] Coke, *Third Institutes*, p. 166.

[51] Coke, *Second Institutes*, I, 228.

[52] Coke, *Third Institutes*, p. 152.

[53] *Ibid.*, p. 205.

[54] R. P., *The Lord Coke His Speech and Charge* (London, 1607). It should be mentioned that R. P. wrote down Sir Edward Coke's charge to the jury at the Norwich Assizes (August, 1606) from memory.

to have taken his stand on the tradition of old England against the dangerous innovations of "modern" times. His favorite religious work seems to have been a *Manipulus Curatorum* of 1496. In the margin of this guide book for priests, Coke jotted down Biblical quotations which might confirm the text of this late medieval work.[55] It is this, the only religious work in his library, which seems to have received more than passing attention. This *Manipulus Curatorum* is not the kind of work which a Puritan would have treasured more than any other guide to spiritual life.

God's law, in Coke's opinion then, could be invoked only for those parts of the law of England which could be documented from scriptural quotations. Clearly here the law of God did not play so vital a part in the common law as did the law of reason.

It is obvious that the power of the judges was greatly enhanced by the idea of legal reason, for they were its custodians. Talking about the idea of reasonable time in law, Coke wrote:

. . . [this] shall be adjudged by the discretion of the justices . . . for reasonableness in these cases belongeth to the knowledge of the law. . . . And this being said of time, the like may be said of things uncertain, which ought to be reasonable, for nothing that is contrary to reason is consonant to law.[56]

Here once again we have a broad concept of judicial interpretation.

But if the judges were to have such broad powers, they had to be independent of the coercion of either king or Parliament. This independence was, of course, directed against outside coercion only and not against the law itself, of which the judges were custodians. Judges were not appointed by his majesty to administer justice according to their own will but

[55] *Manipulus Curatorum* (Rouen, 1496). I would like to express my gratitude to W. O. Hassal for his aid in studying Coke's library at Holkham.

[56] Coke, *First Institutes,* chap. viii, sect. 69, lib. I.

according to the law, customs, and manner of England.[57] Coke disapproved as vigorously as did Ellesmere of judges who handle the "common law like tailors." [58] Coke's idea of the independence of judges was thus a keystone in the whole concept of a law based on legal reason.

James's view of his judicial functions, on the other hand, was a part of his theory of sovereignty. "Kings are properly judges for [kings] sit in the throne of God and thence all judgment is derived." [59] But there was hardly anyone who would deny to the king his ancient attributes as the "fountain of justice." Coke himself, in Cawdrey's case, made the sweeping statement that

the kingly head of this body [the Commonwealth] is instituted and furnished with plenary and entire power, prerogative and jurisdiction, to render justice and right to every part and member of this body.[60]

Dalton, too, held that justice and jurisdiction belonged to the king's authority and was given by him to others.[61] As late as 1631, Sir John Walter, by no means a servile devotee of the prerogative, exclaimed that the king might settle an issue because it was ". . . no matter of trade but for the advancement of justice. . . ." [62]

Did the fact that the king was the fountain of justice mean, as James believed, that "As kings borrow their power from God, so judges from kings"? Was it therefore the king's office also to interpret and settle the law of God within his dominions, while the judges were but to interpret the law of the king? [63] To James the idea of the king as the fountain of justice seemed to connote, in turn, the concept of the king as supreme

[57] R. P., *The Lord Coke His Speech and Charge* (London, 1607), p. 5.
[58] El. 475.
[59] James I, "Speech in Star Chamber, 1616," p. 326.
[60] Coke, *Reports etc.*, 77, 10, Cawdrey's Case.
[61] Dalton, *The Justice of the Peace etc.*, p. 18.
[62] Sir John Walter in *Commons Debates, 1621*, ed. Notestein, Relf, Simpson, IV, 172.
[63] James I, "Speech in Star Chamber 1616," p. 327.

arbiter of the law as a whole. We have already seen how this fitted in with his theory of the prerogative.[64] In James's opinion the law of reason was in his custody and not in the hands of the judges. Such an idea destroyed the effectiveness of the common law as a limitation on the power of the king. No one could deny that the king was the fountain of law; the question was in what manner that power was to be delegated to the judges.

Some who believed in the concept of the law of reason, such as Ellesmere, would make the king the interpreter of this reason. Typically enough, Ellesmere himself was far from clear or decided on this point: in the civil law some say *rex est lex loquens;*

And in this I would not be misunderstood as though I spake of making new laws, or of altering the laws now standing: I mean not so but speak only of interpretation of the law in new questions and doubts. . . .

Was such a shadowy distinction between alteration and interpretation justifiable? It must be remembered that Coke himself did not think that he was "altering" law through bringing it into conformity with reason. As we discussed above, there was a presumption of reasonableness where any act of Parliament was concerned. It must be always kept in mind that, for Coke, ". . . one act of Parliament is *instare omnium* being a proof of the unanswerable and highest nature. . . ." [65] Ellesmere went on to say, however, that while he did not mean to derogate anything from the High Court of Parliament, nevertheless the king had reserved unto himself the supreme power to call Parliament together.[66] Here indeed seems to be the idea that the king was sovereign after all, for in a manner of speaking he was above the highest court of the realm. "Salus populi salus Regis." [67]

[64] *Vide supra*, chap. iii.
[65] Coke, *Fourth Institutes*, IV, 341.
[66] Case of Post Nati, *State Trials etc.*, II, 653-654.
[67] El. 451.

At one council meeting Ellesmere agreed with Coke that the crown's interests must be advanced by lawful rather than by unlawful means and, though a prominent advocate of the union of Scotland and England, he counseled strongly against the infringements of the individual laws of either nation.[68] But it is clear that the Lord Chancellor's support of the ancient laws and customs rested, at least in part, upon utilitarian foundations. His statement that "nothing breeds amongst people such pertinacity in holding on to their customs as sudden and violent efforts to remove them" smacks strongly of Machiavelli's *Il Principe*, for whose author Ellesmere, like Bacon, had a good word to say when it suited his purpose.[69]

Perhaps a unifying force in the Lord Chancellor's thought was his opposition to Coke's idea of judicial interpretation in the name of reason. Reason and interpretation were matters of equity and lately the judges had taken it upon themselves to make orders in equity without regarding the strict rules of law, concerning themselves instead with their implications.[70] Like James he emphasized the judges' function as advisers to the king upon points of law. When, as in the matter of impositions, the judges were unwilling to commit themselves, Ellesmere noted angrily, "the judges are not for a disputant but to judge." [71] It is clear that for Ellesmere such interpretation of the law as there was "in new questions and doubts" was for the king's Chancellor to handle and not for the common law judges. Reason to him seems to have been confined to such "new questions and doubts," traditionally the Chancellor's prerogative. The wider meaning of the law of reason he seems to have ignored. Yet, as we saw, when in doubt he did want to return to reason; a reason, moreover, which had to be arrived at by study and learning.

But this was not Sir Edward Coke's reason. Perhaps we can

[68] *A Brief Discourse Touching the Happy Union of the Kingdoms of England and Scotland* (n. d.). El. 34/B/45 II.

[69] *Ibid.*

[70] El. 2623.

[71] El. 2607.

get a hint of what Ellesmere thought of reason as superior law through his idea of natural law, which he expressed in connection with his plea for the union of England and Scotland. Natural law was a concept drawn out of nature herself. Persian kings are instructed how to apply nature to politics.[72] Natural law, then, was simply the rules of nature applied to politics, rather than something protecting the common law through reason. Thus the king could have reason, with a little study, as well as Sir Edward Coke, though Ellesmere never seems to have stated this point as bluntly as Bacon was to do. His accusations against Coke in Bonham's case were founded on the belief that the judges were prone to "handle the common law like tailors," while new questions and doubts should be settled, as they always had been, by equity through the Chancellor. For Coke's concept of reason as allowing judicial interpretation Ellesmere seems to have shown no more understanding than did his royal master. Here, as in Bacon, Coke's efforts to reinvigorate this concept on behalf of the common law in an age of competing claims to absolute sovereignty were cast aside, while in the practical affairs of the king's council the Lord Chancellor is seen to agree with Coke "in toto" as late as 1616.[73]

Bacon's views on the king's judicial powers were more clearly expressed than were Ellesmere's. With Bacon the king was clearly the custodian of the *legale rationem*. Bacon's views sprang logically from the fact of the king's judicial power. It was impossible for the king to divest himself of any part of his prerogative. To judge and to do justice was an essential part of this prerogative.[74] It follows that the king could not delegate to the judges any independent power. The judges were thus the "twelve lions supporting Solomon's throne," without any independence from the modern "Solomon." Bacon, like James, put great emphasis on the judge's oath, which required men to

[72] *A Brief Discourse etc.*, p. 1.

[73] El. 441.

[74] Bacon, "De Rege Inconsulto," *Works*, ed. Spedding and Heath (1892), VII, 688,

"council" the king.[75] Indeed, James was the "absolute Prince in judicature that hath been in the Christian world." [76] He was also, of course, the originator of all courts.[77] Bacon's argument was not completely divorced from the thought of the times, even so far as the opponents of the king's power were concerned. Was it not one of the prime arguments against the monopolists that they were usurping part of the king's "inseparable prerogative"? That monopolies were illegal because the king could not divest himself of his prerogatives? [78] Could the same argument not hold good for his judicial prerogative as well?

Indeed, Puritans like Nathaniel Carpenter, the author of a pamphlet on wicked politicians, offered an argument not wholly out of tune with Bacon's reasoning. Obedience is due to our superiors "except when [the magistrate] pretends a title to any part of the divine prerogative." [79] By omitting the "divine" we have Bacon's argument. Yet Bacon here, too, showed that inconsistency which we have noted in analyzing his theory of sovereignty. He, like Coke, believed in the doctrine of legal reason and natural law. ". . . Our law is grounded upon the law of nature: from which flows preservation of life natural, liberty which every beast or bird seeketh. . . . National and civil laws which abridge laws of nature therefore to be taken strictly." [80] Yet, in conformity with his general ideas on sover-

[75] Bacon, "Tracts relating to Commendams," *Works*, ed. Montagu (1827), VII, 333. There is some historical justification for the views of justices' functions held by James and Bacon. Until the middle of Henry III's reign the chief justiciar had acted as a prime minister advising the king. See "Justice or Judge" by T. F. Tout, *Dictionary of English History*, ed. Sir Sidney Low and F. S. Pulling (London: Cassel and Co., 1884).

[76] Bacon, *Works*, ed. Montagu (1827), VII, 244.

[77] Bacon, "The Use of the Law," *Works*, ed. Spedding and Heath (1892), VII, 465 ff.

[78] "It is against the Law to communicate the King's Prerogative." *Commons Debates*, 1621, ed. Notestein, Relf, Simpson, IV, 125; also Sir Dudley Digges: "The effects of prerogative in their own nature are noble effects. But when such men have to do with it they beget nothing but Monsters." *Ibid.*, IV, 94.

[79] Nathaniel Carpenter, *Architophel or the Picture of a Wicked Politician* (London, 1629), p. 50.

[80] Bacon in Case of Post Nati, *State Trials etc.*, II, 594–595.

eignty, the king was the "sovereign" in the last resort. For judges, obedience was better than sacrifice.[81] There was in his scheme of things no independent judiciary guarding either the law of nature or the law of reason with their noble precepts.

To Bacon, Coke opposed his concept of the judges' delegated powers,

for all matters of judicature and proceedings in law are distributed to courts of justice, and the king doth judge by his justices.[82]

Again, he wrote, ". . . and the king hath wholly left matters of judicature according to his laws to his judges." [83] He would limit the king even in the appointment of judges, for none could be constituted a judge of the Court of Common Pleas unless he be a sergeant at law of the degree of the coif.[84] It was surely not without a little envy that Coke pointed out how the office of chief baron of the exchequer was granted *quam diu se bene gesserit*

Wherein he hath a more fixed estate (it being an estate for life) than the justices of either bench who have their offices but at will. . . .[85]

The fact that in court the kings sit in high bench did not mean that they were actually to judge themselves. ". . . but judicature only belongeth to the judges of that court, and in his [the king's] presence they answer all motions." [86] In causes both temporal and ecclesiastical the king judges and determines by the "mouth" of the judges.[87] Here the judicial power itself was delegated to the judges. They actually possessed a part of the prerogative; in short, *"Judex est lex loquens."* [88]

[81] Bacon, "De Rege Inconsulto," *Works,* ed. Spedding and Heath (1892), VII, 724.
[82] Coke, *Second Institutes,* I, 186.
[83] Coke, *Fourth Institutes,* p. 70.
[84] *Ibid.,* p. 99.
[85] *Ibid.,* p. 117.
[86] *Ibid.,* p. 73.
[87] Coke, *Reports etc.,* LXXVII, 11, Cawdrey's Case.
[88] Case of Post Nati, *State Trials etc.,* II, 613.

The king must delegate part of his prerogative to the judges, but on the other hand, "no judge of England can make a deputy." [89] This does not mean that the judges themselves were free to pursue their own fancy. They were the solemn custodians of legal reason for ". . . Judges of Record, ought only to see with judicial eyes . . . [not private ones]." [90] Indeed, it was no part of the king's office to decide the *meum et tuum* among his subjects, as James believed.[91] Here, as in the concept of the law of reason, Coke and the common lawyers were in the medieval tradition. Legal reason prescribed the "certainty" of possessions, subject, to be sure, to Parliament's superior judgment on such questions. It held that where there was a wrong committed there must be a remedy. The judges were the custodians of "right," which was synonymous with law and reason. They even attempted to bring parliamentary statutes into line with this concept. Would it be too much to say that here we still have the old saying, ". . . to the king, authority over all, to private persons, property"?

It was the common law or reason which in general divided the two spheres of influence, with the judges as arbiters, subject to Parliament's authority. It was no mere search for ancient authorities which led Coke to Fortescue.

Some actions where either king or subject is sole party . . . [the monarch] can pardon. . . . Yet some he cannot, *i.e.* common nuisances.

And Coke went on to quote Fortescue's similar decision in the matter of repairing a bridge.[92] Here was a meeting of minds, the medieval tradition living on in the age of competition for sovereignty. For Coke, at least, legal reason was in many ways the old natural law writ large. The fact of parliamentary power

[89] *Commons Debates*, 1621, ed. Notestein, Relf, Simpson, II, 316.
[90] Coke, *Reports etc.*, LXXVII, 6, Cawdrey's Case.
[91] James I, "Basilikon Doron," in *Works*, p. 22.
[92] Coke, *Third Institutes*, p. 237. Nicholas Fuller also cites the case of a bridge to prove that the king cannot pardon anything to the "hurt of the subject." *The Argument of Master Nicholas Fuller in the Case of Thomas Land and Richard Mansell etc.* (London, 1607), p. 14.

remained however, not because it was a legislative body, but because it was the highest court.[93]

2

Sir Edward Coke has loomed large in these pages. In his person he sums up the stand of the common law. It is well, therefore, to consider his principal ideas in order to understand more completely the position of the common law as opposed to the new forces at work in the constitution.

Coke's thought has generally been treated in conjunction with the concept of fundamental law. Indeed, "once seized, the idea of fundamental law became the groundwork of most political writing of the time," and most of the political writings during the time of the civil war seemed in one way or another to be concerned with this concept.[94] Coke used the term "fundamental law" frequently in his writings. Magna Carta is the "fountain of all the fundamental laws of the realm, and therefore it may truly be said that it is *magnum in parvo.*" [95] And again, Coke's famous exclamation in the Parliament of 1629, "Magna Carta is such a fellow, that he will have no sovereign," [96] drives home this point. Is the Magna Carta, then, for Coke synonymous with the idea of fundamental law?

There is one striking similarity in all of Coke's assertions as to the place of Magna Carta as fundamental law; this is the stress on Parliament's part in the confirmation of the Charter.

The highest and most binding laws are the statutes which are established by Parliament and by authority of that highest court it is enacted . . . that if any statute be made contrary to the great charter or the charter of the forests it shall be holden for none.[97]

[93] C. H. McIlwain, *The High Court of Parliament etc.* (New Haven: Yale University Press, 1934), p. 84.

[94] See Margaret A. Judson, "Growth of the Theory of Parliamentary Sovereignty in England, 1640–1660" (doctoral thesis, Harvard University, 1935).

[95] Coke, *First Institutes*, chap. iv, sect. 108, lib. 2.

[96] Quoted in McIlwain, *The High Court of Parliament etc.*, p. 83.

[97] Coke, *Second Institutes*, "A Proeme." See also *Commons Debates, 1621*, ed. Notestein, Relf, Simpson, IV, 124.

Was this supposed to mean that Parliament had bound itself for all time, that even if it saw fit to make a "judgment" contrary to the Magna Carta, such a judgment would be void? Indirectly Coke, at least, seemed to concede that this binding of Parliament was voluntary: ". . . all former statutes against either of those charters are now repealed. . . ." [98] This seems to imply that such statutes might have had force while they were standing. Even more significant of Coke's attitude toward Magna Carta as fundamental law is the fact that the statute itself was to him affirmative of the common law, and such act of Parliament, Coke held, did not take away a custom. Indeed, a custom can be prescribed as against such a statute.[99]

The Charter thus is merely declaratory of the ancient laws and liberties of England.[100] What if Parliament had promulgated a negative statute against the Great Charter, would such a statute have been void in Coke's view?

Of the power and jurisdiction of Parliament for making laws in proceeding by bill, it is transcendent and absolute, as it cannot be confined either for causes or persons within any bonds.[101]

Was Magna Carta so sovereign as to confine it?

Magna Carta was, to Coke, fundamental law not of itself but only as it affirmed the ancient laws of England. The law of England was *rectum* because it was the "best birthright a subject has: for thereby his goods, life, honour, lands, wife, etc. are protected from injury and wrong." [102] Law was the "surest sanctuary of all." [103] It was this law which protected the inheritance of Englishmen. What then of Parliament? Was the common law in its turn sovereign in the sense that Parliament was bound to respect it on all occasions?

Coke seems never to have faced this issue squarely. There

[98] Coke, *Second Institutes*, "A Proeme."
[99] Coke, *First Institutes*, chap. x, sect. 170, lib. II.
[100] Coke, *Second Institutes*, I, 2.
[101] Coke, *Fourth Institutes*, p. 36.
[102] Coke, *Second Institutes*, I, 56.
[103] *Ibid.*, p. 55.

was no reason why he should have done so. It was the king and not the Parliament who, in his eyes, sought to subvert the ancient laws of England. Indeed, as the Highest Court of Justice in England, Parliament was an integral part of the ancient laws themselves. "That one act of Parliament is *instare omnium* being a proof of the unanswerable and the highest nature. . . ."[104] Again here we recur to the repetition by Coke of St. Germain's phrase that

. . . it cannot be thought that a statute that is made by the authority of the whole realm . . . will recite a thing against the truth.[105]

As we saw above, the judges saw to it that acts of Parliament did not violate too flagrantly the concept of "reason" on which, in their opinion, the common law was built.

Yet we do have here some elements of contradiction. On the one hand, ". . . Possession is derived from *pos* and *sedeo* because he who is in possession may sit down in rest and quiet." [106] On the other hand Parliament passed the Statute of Uses and sanctioned the dissolution of the monasteries. Indeed, as we have noted, all that Coke could say about statutes restricting trade was that "they never last long." [107] Coke once said about a judgment by a court of justice that it was against the law, but he could hardly have said the same about the judgment of the High Court of Parliament.[108] This, however, need not mean that Coke believed in the sovereignty of Parliament as such. We saw him draw back when Parliament began to exceed its powers by invading the prerogative of foreign affairs. We saw him draw back again when the Commons was in danger of exceeding its jurisdiction.

The king in all his weighty affairs had used the advice of his Lords and Commons . . . always provided that both Lords and

[104] Coke, *Fourth Institutes*, p. 341.
[105] *Ibid.*, p. 342.
[106] Coke, *Reports etc.*, LXXVII, 340, Brediman's Case.
[107] For a discussion of this problem, *vide infra*, chap. iv.
[108] Coke, *Second Institutes*, I, 62.

Commons keep themselves within the circle of the laws and customs of Parliament.[109]

Here is no theory of parliamentary omnicompetence. After all, even Fortescue had regarded statutes as binding.[110]

The term "fundamental law," then, did not mean to Coke the sovereignty of the common law as against both Parliament and king. But it did not mean the sovereignty of Parliament either, which must keep itself within the circle of its own laws and customs.[111] Nor, of course, did the term imply the sovereignty of the king. Fundamental law here seems not too far removed from Fortescue's *dominium politicum et regale*. The diverse parts of the English polity were held together, and their boundaries defined, by the law. The phrase *"legem terrae"* in Magna Carta is significant, Coke tells us:

> And it is not said *legem et consuetudinem regis Angliae*, lest it might be thought to bind the king only, nor *populi Angliae*, lest it might be thought to bind them only, but that the law might extend to all, it is said *per legem terrae Angliae*.[112]

Sir John Fortescue had defined law as derived from "ligando," for the body mystical is held together by the law as the body physical is held together by the nerves. Nearly a century and a half later, Coke comments upon this passage in his copy of the *De Laudibus Legum Angliae*, *"lex, lex, nota, nota."* [113] Fortescue's high regard for the vital function of the law was received with undisguised enthusiasm by Sir Edward Coke. To Coke Magna Carta was fundamental law not in the sense of sovereignty but in that it symbolized the fact that the fundamental constitution of England was a *dominium politicum et regale*.

Yet it must be added that there were times when Coke came very close to conceding great powers to Parliament. Eventu-

---

[109] Coke, *Fourth Institutes*, p. 35.

[110] *Vide supra*, chap. i.

[111] *I.e.*, Coke, *First Institutes*, chap. x, sect. 164, lib. II.

[112] Coke, *Second Institutes*, I, 50.

[113] Sir John Fortescue, *De Laudibus Legum Angliae* (London, 1546), folio XVI.

ally, perhaps, he came to realize that Parliament was the most effective bulwark against the king's pretensions, which would have torn asunder the ancient order of the English polity, an order of which the binding force of statutes was a part. The common law so admeasured the prerogative of kings that they could not prejudice the inheritance of any man.[114] The term "inheritance" covered all of the ancient rights and liberties of the subject. The king could not change any part of the common law nor create an offense which was not an offense before.[115] After all, the law must not be hindered in its function of giving everyone his due; ". . . want of right and want of remedy are in one equipage." [116]

Here we seem to be back with Fortescue. It was to him a vital part of the superior law of nature that it granted to everyone his due.[117] With him the natural law had protected the inheritance of the subject from arbitrary interference. Coke in turn removed the common law from the purview of the king, if not quite of Parliament. The king might not change any part of the common law by proclamations, nor was he even a judge of the law, though he was the fountain of justice.[118] "The process and execution, which is the life of the law, consisteth in the king's writs," [119] but this did not mean that the king could issue new writs at his leisure. Coke fought the prerogative courts because they jeopardized the independent status of the law. It was one thing for judges "to play the chancellor's part upon the statutes"; it was another thing for the Chancellor to do so himself.

In Chudleigh's case, eight years before Queen Elizabeth's death, the judges had stated that he who has the "use" of land was really not seized with any property at all, for he had no remedy against infringements but in chancery and ". . . the Chancellor has no power to determine the right of inheritance.

[114] Coke, *Second Institutes*, I, 36.
[115] Case of Proclamations, *State Trials etc.*, II, 726-727.
[116] Coke, *Reports etc.*, LXXVI, 342, Brediman's Case.
[117] *Vide supra*, chap. i.
[118] Case of Proclamations, *State Trials etc.*, II, 727.
[119] Coke, *First Institutes*, chap. xi, sect. 199, lib. II.

..." [120] For Coke, too, the chancery could meddle with nothing that could be determined at common law.[121] Indeed only certain specific matters could be judged in that court of "conscience"; frauds and deceits, accidents, breach of trust and confidence.[122] None of these touch deeply upon the inheritance of the subject. Similarly Coke would confine and limit the jurisdictions of the other prerogative courts.[123] The danger of want of remedy against injustice, which he felt sometimes characterized the chancery, must be avoided.[124] To be fined at the king's will did not mean to be punished by arbitrary power, but that the king's justices shall set the fine, according to the ancient laws of England.[125]

When the law gave anything to a man, it also implicitly gave whatever was necessary for taking and enjoying the same. No arbitrary power could interfere. A tenant at will, for example, could not be evicted at the pleasure of the lessor. He must be able to reap the crop which he sowed, even if he should be evicted before the harvest.[126] Every Englishman had positive rights, "and well may the laws of England be called libertates, quia Liberos faciunt." [127]

Coke went to great lengths in this respect. As in Fortescue, the king could not pardon common nuisances, since he could dispense only with his own part in the matter of fines, but not with the part of the aggrieved party.[128] Acts of Parliament might even limit the king's pardoning powers, and Coke but grudgingly admitted that it had been held that the king

---

[120] Coke, *Reports etc.*, LXXVI, 278, Chudleigh's Case.

[121] *Commons Debates*, 1621, ed. Notestein, Relf, Simpson, II, 265.

[122] Coke, *Fourth Institutes*, p. 84.

[123] *Ibid.*, p. 97. The Star Chamber, "the most honorable court in the Christian world, our Parliament excepted," should confine itself to its just jurisdiction, which observed will keep all England quiet, p. 65. For ecclesiastical courts see, for example, Coke, *Reports etc.*, LXXVI, 77, 288, Marquess of Winchester's Case.

[124] *Commons Debates*, 1621, ed. Notestein, Relf, Simpson, II, 233.

[125] Coke, *Second Institutes*, I, 168.

[126] Coke, *First Institutes*, chap. viii, sect. 68, lib. I.

[127] *Ibid.*, chap. iv, sect. 108, lib. II.

[128] Coke, *Third Institutes*, p. 237.

could dispense with such acts by a *non obstante*.[129] Coke went even further: in matters of defense of the realm, the subjects' inheritances were scrupulously guarded. Fortescue had conceded to the king power over all matters in emergencies.[130] Could the king take saltpeter for gunpowder from the subject's lands? Yes, because the safety and defense of the realm were the concern of the king—but in so doing he had to observe the rights of the subjects. The place dug must be repaired so that it was left in good condition. The king had but purveyance and could not restrain the owner from digging the saltpeter himself, "for the property thereof is in the owner of the soil." [131] Even here the inheritance of the subject was scrupulously safeguarded against the king.

Enough has been said to show that here we have the old *ius*, the positive rights of the subject. Such rights are not in tune with any theory of complete sovereignty.

Yet Coke very scrupulously safeguarded the lawful prerogatives of the king. These prerogatives Coke found in the ancient laws. The levying of war and matters of foreign policy are the king's prerogatives. Coke later was to waver in regard to Parliament's authority in matters of state.[132] The ancient rights of the crown should be safeguarded, especially with respect to finances. It was the treasurer's duty to see that these sources of income not be depleted. Fortescue, too, was concerned to keep the royal domain intact.[133] In tune with his medieval predecessors, Coke held that "ordinary charges the king should bear alone but *ubi commune periculum, commune auxilium*." [134] But *commune auxilium* did not mean, as even Fortescue would have it mean, that in an emergency the king was

---

[129] *Ibid.*, p. 235.

[130] *Vide supra*, chap. i.

[131] Coke, *Third Institutes*, pp. 83-84.

[132] *Commons Debates*, 1621, ed. Notestein, Relf, Simpson, II, 230; for Coke's more extreme view, see pp. 541-542; see also, Coke, *Third Institutes*, p. 9: "To the King only belongs the authority to levy war, in subjects it is High Treason."

[133] Coke, *Fourth Institutes*, p. 104.

[134] *Parliamentary Debates*, 1623, ed. Gardiner (1873), p. 32.

absolute. "The Lords and Commons cannot be charged with anything for the defense of the realm . . . unless it be by their will in Parliament. . . ." [135] The *meum et tuum* was outside the reach of the king. His council should concern itself with public matters only.[136] On the other hand, the king was the "*caput principium et finis*" of Parliament: he could prorogue and adjourn it.[137] Coke voiced a pious hope that Parliament should be held once a year.[138]

There were other miscellaneous prerogatives: forfeitures on penal laws, the raising of beacons and lighthouses on the high seas.[139] These prerogatives Sir Edward Coke was careful to preserve for the king. They were an intrinsic part of the English polity. When Parliament started to interfere with the power of war and peace, Coke exclaimed about a petition upon these subjects:

> If it were petition of right which requires answer, I would never prefer it. Marriages, leagues, war and peace *arcana imperii*. . . . But it's only a petition of grace.[140]

England to him was still essentially a *dominium politicum et regale*.

There was here, as with Fortescue, no conflict between the pre-eminent position of king and the people's rights. "The king who is God's annointed . . . as having his power derived from God within his territories," did not mean to Coke as it did to James that he was *solutus legibus* as well.[141] However, Coke's argument in the case of the Post Nati comes very close to constituting a realization of the meaning of sovereignty. If there were no sovereign to prescribe laws and no people of allegiance to obey them, there could be no laws made or executed. "By

---

[135] Coke, *Second Institutes*, I, 61.

[136] Coke, *Fourth Institutes*, p. 52.

[137] *Ibid.*, pp. 2, 9.

[138] *Ibid.*, p. 9.

[139] *Commons Debates*, 1621, ed. Notestein, Relf, Simpson, II, 228-229.

[140] *Ibid.*, II, 495.

[141] Trial of the Conspirators in the Gun Powder Plot, *State Trials etc.*, II, 176.

which it appears that between sovereignty and allegiance laws are begotten." [142]

Coke was here concerned to prove that the king's allegiance extended beyond the confines of his territory. He went on to cite as an example the Statute Prerogativa Regis as well as the fact that subjects of the kings of Portugal and of other continental monarchs were bound to defend their countries, even if they did not live within its confines.[143] But Coke did not proceed, as Raleigh might have done, to equate the English polity with those on the continent. The laws which the sovereign might have prescribed originally were the laws of England by which he could not prejudice the inheritance of any. Similarly Coke wrote:

. . . all the lands within this realm were originally derived from the crown, and therefore the king is sovereign lord or lord paramount, either mediate or immediate of all and every parcel of land within the realm.[144]

Nevertheless, not even the tenant at will could be deprived by any lessor without recompense. The headship of the king did not exclude the rights of the subjects.

Coke seemed to have realized that this theory of the constitution had medieval roots. He supplied numerous examples of abuses which had only recently crept upon the ancient laws and institutions of England. Gaolers and coroners could now take money from subjects.[145] Defendants no longer had to appear in court in person, but could be represented by attorneys. The result of this was the multiplication of suits.[146] New courts, new offices had been created, not to speak of trading corporations which hindered free trade and traffic.[147]

Coke was fighting against a rising tide. He professed his own

[142] Case of Post Nati, *ibid.*, II, 570.
[143] *Ibid.*, II, 570-571.
[144] Coke, *First Institutes*, sect. 85, lib. II.
[145] Coke, *Second Institutes*, I, 73-74.
[146] *Ibid.*, I, 249.
[147] *Ibid.*, II, 540.

impotence against parliamentary restrictions on free trade. Nor was it a solution to offer a thousand pounds as a "private man" to stop the growing demands for money on the part of the crown, demands which were undermining the harmony of the commonwealth.[148]

Coke was also aware of the danger of equating England with continental monarchies. We have seen how royalist writers tended to do just this, while Parliament fought against it. "And here it is worthy of consideration," Coke wrote,

> . . . how the laws of England are not derived from any foreign law, either canon, civil, or other, but a special law appropriated to this kingdom, and most accommodate and apt for the good government thereof.[149]

To which the Jesuit pamphleteer Robert Parsons queried in answer to Coke:

> Do not subjects in Scotland, France, Italy, Spain . . . enjoy peace and quietness . . . as well by their laws imperial as we do by our municipal? [150]

Parsons attacked Coke in much the same way as James, Raleigh, or other royalist writers might have done. His accusations were based, in the last resort, on a lack of understanding of the medieval English constitution. He had, obviously, not read his Fortescue. Laws well executed by a prince were to him more important than written law. Bacon too had exclaimed, *"Optimus magistratus praestat optimae lege."* [151] The prince may administer justice by the laws of nature and of nations, Parsons asserted. Had not Coke, he continued, even admitted that the king gave life to the law?[152]

Sir Edward Coke himself would gladly have admitted the

---

[148] *Commons Debates,* 1625, ed. Gardiner (1873), p. 100.

[149] Coke, *Third Institutes,* p. 100.

[150] Robert Parsons, *An Answer etc.* (n.p., 1606), p. 14.

[151] Bacon, "Speech on taking his place in Chancery (1617)," *Works,* ed. Montagu (1827), VII, 257.

[152] Robert Parsons, *An Answer etc.* (n.p., 1606), p. 14.

latter part of Parson's statement—not only was the king the supreme judge but he was also the "fountain of law." But both of these attributes were exercised for him either by his justices or by the King in Parliament, of which he was *caput et finis*. To Parsons these may have been shadowy distinctions, for he showed plainly that he was not acquainted with the idea of legal reason which for Coke underlay the common law as the sinews of the commonwealth. "Their common law, which pretendeth to follow reason," he said contemptuously.[153] *Ius* to him was not bound up with the principles of the common law grounded on legal reason, which had to be learned and studied before it could be understood. He even accused Coke of confusing *lex* with *ius*, and here again Coke would have admitted the justice of the accusation.[154] For to Parsons *ius* had the much broader connotation of *bonum et aequum*,[155] and such a broad concept of *ius* was the very idea which the common lawyers had to combat. It would have brought the inheritances of Englishmen within the compass of the king's, and indeed of any man's judgment.

James, as we have seen, tried to broaden the idea of legal reason in just such a way, in order that he might encompass it. Nor is Parsons' coupling of the law of nature with the law of nations without significance. On at least one occasion Coke was careful to distinguish the two.[156] Would this equation of the *ius gentium*, with its Roman law connotation, to the law of nature not lead eventually to invidious comparisons of England with continental nations? It did with Parsons. Small wonder, then, that Parsons finally attacked Coke's praise of the antiquity of English law. Basing himself on history, he pointed out that the laws of England arose from the Conquest and were meant to bridle the English, as could be seen by the constant clamor for the laws of King Edward's time.[157] Parsons may have had

[153] *Ibid.*, p. 14.
[154] *Ibid.*, p. 2.
[155] *Ibid.*
[156] Coke, *First Institutes*, chap. ii, sect. 172, lib. II, The Origin of Villeinage.
[157] Parsons, *An Answer etc.*, pp. 15, 16.

some historical justification. But here Coke was not praising the ancient laws of England for themselves, but as symbols, like Magna Carta, of the ancient English polity, the *dominium politicum et regale,* which knew no clear sovereignty. For that polity Robert Parsons, the exile, had little understanding—no more than had James, the Scotsman.

Yet even in Coke there are glimpses not found in Fortescue. How far was his legal reason identical with the earlier natural law? Were acts of Parliament merely declaratory of legal reason, the basic principle of the common law? We have seen earlier how the presumption of reason underlay acts of Parliament.[158] But then there had been acts of Parliament promulgated against the Great Charter (though they were now happily repealed), there had been bills interfering with the freedom of trade. Even Parliament's jurisdiction over property had been rationalized and assimilated, and those decisions were reported by Coke without disagreement.[159] Would it be nearer the point to link Coke to St. Germain rather than to Fortescue? On the other hand there were royal prerogatives which to Coke were *arcana imperii.* But these *arcana imperii* never interfered with the subjects' inheritances.

In the thought of Sir Edward Coke, then, we find summed up the stand and the dilemma of the common lawyers in an age of competition for sovereignty. There is little doubt that Coke's ideal was that of a continuous and harmonious commonwealth, a *dominium politicum et regale.* Yet he had to deal with the rising tide of parliamentary power. At one occasion he asserted, as we observed earlier, that Parliament might treat of anything: state matters and matters concerning Church and government. Yet Parliament was not, to him, properly speaking, sovereign, no more than were the common law or Magna Carta. Indeed, he was doubtful whether Parliament could deal with foreign affairs because this was a matter of government. In the last resort he had to concede, however, the overriding power of statutes, though he, like St. Germain, could take

---

[158] *Vide supra,* p. 143.
[159] See the diverse statutes dealing with uses, *vide supra,* chap. iv.

refuge behind the idea that the representatives of the whole realm would never decide anything against the truth, a truth largely to be determined by the judges through the idea of legal reason. But here again no legal reason could presumably destroy entirely such statutes as, for example, those restricting trade, a principle not congenial to the common law. Acquiescence in the judgment of the High Court was all that was possible.

Coke's thought does not have the clarity and consistency of Sir John Fortescue's. It is only natural that this should be the case, for Coke lived in a time marked by the transition from one concept of the constitution to another. The *dominium politicum et regale* was yielding to the sovereignty of the King in Parliament. Meanwhile, on his own account, the king was making his bid for complete sovereignty. Between the two competing sovereignties of the king without Parliament and of the King in Parliament, Sir Edward Coke and the common lawyers were on the defensive, trying to preserve the harmonious spirit of the medieval constitution.

In Coke's lifetime the king rather than the Parliament seemed to advance a theory of sovereignty which presented the greater menace to the liberties of Englishmen. Indeed, it must have seemed, at the moment, that Parliament in fighting the king was standing on the traditional ground of the constitution rather than itself elaborating a rival concept of sovereignty.[160] Moreover, as we have already indicated, the courts had gone far toward recognizing Parliament's power over matters such as property at a time when Coke was but a young man. It was no small wonder, then, that Coke in the end sided with Parliament while trying to preserve the traditional concept of the constitution.

We do not as yet have sufficient evidence to determine if Coke fully realized the importance of the pretensions of Parlia-

[160] Margaret A. Judson stresses the traditionalism of the Commons in her *The Crisis of the Constitution* (New Brunswick: Rutgers University Press, 1949).

ment as constituting in themselves a menace to his concept of the commonwealth. Fundamentally Coke was in the position of our modern liberals: constantly on the defensive, he had to maintain the middle road between the two new doctrines, both of which were challenging the liberties of Englishmen as he and his predecessors had conceived them. It is therefore profoundly erroneous to characterize Coke as "harsh, avaricious and narrow." The defense of the *dominium politicum et regale* was bound to lead to such acts as the fierce prosecution of Raleigh to prevent what looked like treason against the king, the head of the commonwealth. It also involved the defiance of the king on legal grounds when he in turn sought to grasp a greater sovereignty. Eventually it signified participation on the side of Parliament in the struggle against the king's pretensions, even though such participation might lead to an enhancing of the equally absolute claim to sovereignty on the part of the King in Parliament. In public life Coke was above all a fighter, albeit in a lost cause. It was a fighting spirit which imbued him with an instinctive and uncompromising reverence for the law. It is interesting to note that a nineteenth-century liberal like the historian John Richard Green could blame Coke on this count, in spite of the fact that the great common lawyer's narrowness was exercised in the name of a middle road which would preserve the liberty of the individual against all arbitrary power.[161]

Coke and the common lawyers thus preserved something of the old spirit of the constitution in an age of increasing competition for sovereignty. This tradition was to survive even in the stormy times of the revolution. It is outside the scope of this essay to trace its further course. Yet a man like Sir Roger Twysden, living during the Civil War, typifies its continuity: he, like Coke, knew no "sovereignty." He refused to pay ship money to the king, refused a loan to the Long Parliament, and resigned his office rather than burden his county with coat

[161] John Richard Green, *A Short History of the English People* (New York: A. L. Burt, n. d.), II, 35.

money for Cromwell's militia.[162] Was there more nearly perfect expression of Coke's thought than Sir Roger Twysden's concept of the liberty of Englishmen?

> ... it seems to me there is no rule for either the liberty of the subject or the prerogative of the king but the law of the land, which in some sense may be said to be the genus, and they the two distinct species.[163]

Not only was the king limited; even Parliament did not usually meddle with certain issues, though its authority was absolute.[164] Twysden was not alone, for others continued to express the old tradition of the *dominium politicum et regale*, where the law, removed from arbitrary might, cemented the English polity.

The transference of the struggle to the battlefield brought into still sharper focus the dilemma of those who, like the Welsh Judge Jenkins, still believed in the traditional concept of the constitution. Contemplating the England of the Civil War from his prison cell in the Tower, the judge reflected sadly that

> ... the King declares it treason to adhere to the Houses in this war, the Houses declare it treason to adhere to the king. What surer guide to action, therefore, has the subject but the law of the land? [165]

But the defense of this very law had put the old judge behind prison bars, where he was to spend the short remaining months of his life. Even some Puritan radicals were beginning to support Jenkins' position, though on a somewhat different basis. The lives and properties of the subject should be without the reach of "Kingly Royalists" or "Parliamentary Realists." But

[162] Sir Roger Twysden, *The Government of England* (Camden Society, 1849), pp. xxxviii, lxix, lxxxiii, Introduction.

[163] *Ibid.*, p. 83.

[164] *Ibid.*, chap. xvi.

[165] David Jenkins, "Lex Terrae or the Laws of the Land," *Judge Jenkins*, ed. W. H. Terry (London: G. Richards and H. Toulmin, 1929), p. 48.

the foundation for this view was not the law of the land but the scriptural injunction: "Thou shalt not steal." [166] However, the thought of a new age was expressed not by the judge nor by the Puritan, but by their contemporary, Sir Robert Filmer:

We do but flatter ourselves, if we hope ever to be governed without an arbitrary power. No, we mistake, the question is not whether there shall be an arbitrary power, but the only point is who shall have that arbitrary power, whether one or many: there never was, nor never can be a people governed without the power of making laws, and every power of making laws must be arbitrary. . . .[167]

[166] William Ball, *The Rule of a Free-Born People* (n. p., 1646), II, 8.

[167] Sir Robert Filmer, *The Anarchy of a Limited or Mixed Monarchy* (n. p., 1648), preface.

IX

CONCLUSION

†

THE QUESTION NEVER WAS whether we should be governed by
arbitrary power but in whose hands it should be."[1] When Albertus Warren wrote these words the English Revolution was
already twelve years old. Parliament had won its battle against
the king's pretensions. When Charles I had faced the execu-
tioner, the king's attempt to win the undisputed supremacy of
the realm perished with him. The end result of the Revolution
determined Englishmen's preference for parliamentary government over royal absolutism. However, emphasis on the victory of "government by discussion" over "government by the
king" has too often led to the omission of one of the chief determining factors of the Revolution. For the English Revolution was, in the last resort, a struggle for power between two
competing ideas of sovereignty. In the end it was parliamentary
omnicompetence which emerged, even if this was largely to
remain a matter of theory rather than actual fact.

Albertus Warren was as shrewd an observer of the trend of
his times as was Thomas Hobbes, for whoever held the power

[1] Albertus Warren, *Eight Reasons Categorical etc.* (London, 1653), p. 5.

of sword undoubtedly held the whole sovereignty.[2] The actual outbreak of the Civil War was, indeed, bound up with the disputed control over the militia. By the end of the seventeenth century Parliament had the control over the armed forces in its hands. In the late nineteenth century, Dicey was forced to point out that the only external check on the sovereign Parliament was resistance by force, not by law.[3]

What of the common law which had traditionally guaranteed the rights of individuals against arbitrary interference? Looking back over the Revolution, Sir Matthew Hale, writing in the reign of Charles II, exalted the certainty of law against all forms of arbitrary government.[4] Holdsworth contended that the views of the common law and common lawyers triumphed with the victory of Parliament.[5] As long as the judges played the "chancellor's part upon the statutes," Parliament was not completely sovereign.

Was this idea of legal reason in reality an adequate incarnation of the old concept of natural law? We have tried to show how gradually natural law was undermined by the competition for sovereignty. The custodianship of the rights of Englishmen was transferred from the superhuman bosom of natural law to the human bosom of Parliament, in which all men were represented. Even St. Germain's law of reason no longer had the force of Fortescue's natural law. Perhaps Coke's reluctant acquiescence in the omnicompetence of Parliament demonstrates

[2] Thomas Hobbes, "Dialogue of the Common Law," *The English Works of Thomas Hobbes* (hereafter "Dialogue"), ed. W. Molesworth (London, 1849), p. 18. Ernest Cassirer has pointed out the importance of the idea of an absolute power (Machtwille) which gives law to both the Puritans and Hobbes: with the former it is the overriding command of God, with the latter the command of the Leviathan, the "mortal God." *Die Platonische Renaissance in England und die Schule von Cambridge* (Leipzig: G. B. Taubner, 1932), pp. 54-55.

[3] A. V. Dicey, *Introduction to the Study of the Law of the Constitution* (London: Macmillan, 1897), pp. 73, 76.

[4] Sir Matthew Hale, "Reflections by the Lord Chief Justice Hale on Mr. Hobbes' Dialogue of the Law" (hereafter "Reflections"), W. S. Holdsworth, *A History of English Law* (London: Methuen and Co., 1924), V, 509 ff.

[5] W. S. Holdsworth, *History of English Law* (Boston: Little, Brown, 1927), V, 491.

the trend toward sovereignty with greatest clarity. Though the common law "did ever allow free trade," yet there was no way to invalidate acts of Parliament violating this principle. At times Coke even allowed Parliament authority over matters of state.

Nevertheless, the idea of legal reason did make it possible for the lawyers occasionally to bring acts of Parliament into line with this concept, for an act of Parliament seemingly never recited anything against the truth. That we find this statement of Christopher St. Germain's repeated by Coke, is, however, another clear sign of the common lawyer's reluctant acquiescence in the growth of parliamentary sovereignty, as clear as the decisions rationalizing Parliament's control over property.

However, the idea of legal reason could be a source of weakness as well as of strength. It meant that the law and its interpretations would increasingly become a matter for specialists. On the one hand, this removed the law from the king's control, since he was not a member of the Inns of Court; but on the other hand any inquiry into basic postulates of right and justice had to be rejected. We saw how Parsons attacked Coke on the basis that law must conform to *bonum* and *aequum*. Thomas Hobbes was to follow in Parson's footsteps. To the charge that a man is condemned to death for the theft of a few shillings worth of wood, the common lawyer in Hobbes' *Dialogue* can only answer that "It has been so practiced time out of mind." [6] Sir Matthew Hale himself held that inquiries into basic concepts of justice and right were matters for individual judgment only, and beside the point as far as the common law was concerned.[7] Was not the common law the "law by which a kingdom has been governed happily for five hundred years"? [8]

The Revolution was thus but an incident to the great common lawyer, a few decades of strife against five hundred years of peace. Obviously Sir Matthew Hale failed to grasp the signifi-

[6] Hobbes, "Dialogue," p. 94.

[7] Hale, "Reflections," p. 504.

[8] Sir Matthew Hale, *Considerations touching the Amendments of Alterations of Laws, Hargraves Law Tracts* (Dublin, 1787), I, 256-258.

cance of the English Revolution as a struggle for power.[9] The flourishing movements for the reform of the common law might have given him pause, though, at least temporarily, the Restoration swept away any hope for law reform.[10] But surely it was only a matter of time until the inadequacies of the common law would be redressed, in spite of the idea of legal reason, by an almighty Parliament.

Nevertheless, in the age of competition for sovereignty the common lawyers provided almost the only link with the medieval constitution of Sir John Fortescue. Sir Edward Coke, Twysden and Hale later tried to preserve the continuity. If they seem to us to stand on narrow medieval precedent, devoid of much abstract reasoning and speculation, we must never forget that this was the only way the competing sovereignties could be checked. The contrast in what they tried to accomplish and what actually was wrought by the progress of years stands out when we read a statement which Harold Laski made in 1938.

Legally we have no fundamental rights in Great Britain; we trust for their protection to the ordinary constitutional machinery of the state. And in quiet times, we need not doubt that such protection is ample for all necessary purposes. The problem lies in the fact that in periods of rapid social change the substance of what appears fundamental to one sort of opinion does not appear fundamental to another.[11]

This was just what the common lawyers wanted to avoid. That is why they emphasized the certainty of the law. That is why Sir Matthew Hale preferred a certain law, however imperfect, to any kind of arbitrary government.[12] Would they have relished a Parliament whose only external check was resistance

[9] For a more detailed discussion of this point see, George L. Mosse, "Thomas Hobbes: Jurisprudence at the Crossroads," *University of Toronto Quarterly,* XV (July, 1946), 346-355.

[10] Goldwin Smith, "The Reform of the Laws of England," *University of Toronto Quarterly,* X (July, 1941), 480.

[11] Harold Laski, *Parliamentary Government in England* (New York: Viking Press, 1938), p. 41.

[12] Hale, "Reflections," p. 503.

by force? Would they have accepted the uncertain pressure of public opinion as a substitute for a certain law protecting individual rights? And yet parliamentary sovereignty, without Bodin's *droit*, was the outcome of this competition for sovereignty. In spite of the failure of the royalist quest for sovereignty the absolute stage emerged, the privileges of Parliament came to be substituted for the prerogatives of the king as James I had conceived them.[13] It is this assimilation of the idea of sovereignty in English political and constitutional thought which John Austin made the basis for his theory of sovereignty, and which Thomas Hobbes had used before him to conjure up Leviathan, that "mortal" God.

Sir Edward Coke's concept of legal reason, while failing to halt the struggle for sovereignty in England, was, through the concept of judicial review, to provide the citadel of American constitutionalism.[14] In England, over a century after the limits of our analysis, Blackstone was to deride the idea of judicial review as subversive of all government for the legislature should not be controlled by any other power.[15] Here, once more, we see the result of the struggle for sovereignty in England, which marks the transition from the medieval to the modern theory of the constitution.

[13] Wilhelm Kotter, *Der Raetegedanke als Staatsgedanke* (Leipzig: Th. Weicher, 1925), I, 8, 9.

[14] Edward S. Corwin, *Liberty against Government* (Baton Rouge: Louisiana State University Press, 1948), p. 170.

[15] Sir William Blackstone, *Commentaries on the Laws of England*, I, 91, quoted in Francis D. Wormuth, *The Origins of Modern Constitutionalism* (New York: Harpers, 1949), p. 209.

Index

A

Alford, Edward, 26, 113, 118–119, 120, 134, 135
Apology of 1604, 86, 115
Ashley, Sergeant, 121
Austin, John, 1, 2, 179

B

Bacon, Sir Francis, 94, 96, 156
  common law, 75, 141
  higher law, 77, 146
  judges, 80
  the king as judge, 79, 155, 156
  the king and law, 75, 77–78
  law of nature, 156
  legal reason, 156
  Magna Carta, 77–78, 80
  the monarchy, 75
  monopolies, 156
  parliamentary powers, 75, 76
  POLITICAL THOUGHT OF, 74–81, 146–156
  the prerogative, 76–77, 105, 156

  reason of state, 51, 79–80
  Statute of Uses, 101, 103
  Bodin, 80
  Carpenter, 156
  Coke, 77, 156–157
  Machiavelli, 80, 154
Ball, Sir Peter, 46
Ball, William, 174 n.
Bancroft, Archbishop, 91
Bateman, Robert, 97
Bates, case of, 51, 84–89, 128, 133
Blackstone, Sir William, 179
Boccalini, Trajano, 52
Bodin, Jean, 25, 32, 37, 42, 44
  England, 32–33, 39, 93
  law of God, 29
  law of nature, 29–30, 107, 126
  Parliament, 88
  POLITICAL THOUGHT OF, 28–33
  reason of state, 30, 50
  sovereignty, 28–29, 81, 82
  Bacon, 80
  Forsett, 37, 39
  Fortescue, 29–30
  Fullbeck, 34, 36, 37

R